A Life in the Day of a Lady Salesman

A Life in the Day of a Lady Salesman

Diana Amann Cruze

Cruze Books

Cover Design by Geneva Hill

Back cover photo by Judy S. Blackstock

Published by Cruze Books

ISBN-13: 978-1463562311
ISBN-10: 1463562314

Typesetting services by BOOKOW.COM

This book is dedicated to my customers who kept me out of a cubicle throughout thirty-two years of sales.

Acknowledgments

Mary Lee Vix, who always knew when to drain the swamp

Harland Vix, who delivered chemicals and repaired equipment with little or no pay

Don Williams, author and writing teacher extraordinaire, without whose critique I would not have continued writing

Classmates of Don's writing classes who offered comments, encouragement, and laughter

Rich Cole, who first read and critiqued the draft and added invaluable comments

Eleanor Cole, who encouraged me and offered her home as a quiet place for me to work

Cathy Kodra, editor, without whose editing, guidance, and kindness I would have given up on this project (www.cathykodra.com)

Kem Morgan, who read the book's draft and gave much helpful advice and construction

Nancy, sister, who introduced me to Kem, often acting as courier

Wayne, who helped deliver chemicals and often performed inventory duty He supported my effort as it took much longer to finish this book than I had anticipated.

Hugh Kyle, former Venturetech service manager, who formulated products to my specs and answered my never-ending questions with patience and knowledge. Thanks also to Venturetech delivery drivers.

Thanks to:

Peggy Fain, for her photo of Tinsley-Bible Drugstore in Dandridge, TN, Chapter 2

Sonya Garrett of Jamestown, TN, for her photograph of Jamestown, Chapter 15

Roane County Board of Education Transportation Department employees Tim Goss, Matt Russell, and Jackie Teague for permission to photograph them, Chapter 16

Roane County Highway Department employees Joe Britton, Wendell Hamby, and Grant King for permission to photograph them, Chapters 4 and 16

Forest Stiltner for posting the photo of Grundy, VA, Chapter 2 (Photographer unknown)

Ray Fraley, Campbell County Board of Education Maintenance Department, for allowing me to photograph his taxidermy display, Chapter 9

Wolcott, Marion Post, 1910- photographer
Copper mining and sulfuric acid plant, Copperhill, Tenn, 1939;
Title from FSA or OWI agency caption; Transfer from U.S. Office of War Information, 1944, Chapter 16

Many other photographs taken by author

I am grateful to all the people who have been a part of or have helped with this book. Any errors are my own.

Author's Note

The timeline of this book is from 1970 through 2012. Many names have been changed in order to avoid embarrassment to characters I have included. In some instances, I have simply forgotten those names.

Dates and conversations are written as nearly as I could remember, and in some cases composite dialogue is included.

Preface

I slipped through the back door of the school kitchen. Two cooks yelled, "Gladys, the lady salesman is here!" I heard that call often during years of selling to school lunchrooms and other accounts.

Mechanics, secretaries, and purchasing agents alike invariably called me the "Lady Salesman." Perhaps they assigned this label because my outside sales career took place during a time when women were uncommon in sales, other than retail.

Perhaps because I spent my early working life in secretarial positions, I longed for the freedom of any type of work that would allow me to travel. My first taste of this life was a position with a cookie company. I stacked snacks onto a hand truck at the loading dock and wheeled them into the store to price and shelve.

The cookie experience led to a job with a novelty company, delivering and stacking racks with hair products, batteries, and toys. My customers included drugstores, grocery stores, and small hospital gift shops. I traveled to small Appalachian towns in Tennessee, Virginia, West Virginia, Kentucky, and North Carolina.

After a few months with the novelty company, a local business that sold tobacco, candy, and novelties hired me for a route position. The tobacco company assigned me an area in East Tennessee only, and I missed the rest of southern Appalachia, where I had traveled with two previous jobs. Two years of selling tobacco led to an offer from a business that sold groceries to restaurants, schools, and any industry that served food. Knoxville and surrounding counties now comprised my sales territory.

The routine of food sales soon offered mostly tedium. Managers of my company split my territory, costing me much of my commission. I left the company to accept a position in chemical sales so that traveling in these mountains would be possible again. In 1994, I started my own company, Amann Industries. Most dealings with customers involved loading my vehicle with products and a hand truck for deliveries to businesses in Tennessee and Kentucky.

I retired in 2006, but later accepted a position with a local chemical company. I retired with finality in 2009. I then began to write about my travels, using notes jotted and saved during thirty-two years in sales.

Diana at five years old

Introduction

In three words I can sum up everything I've learned about life: it goes on.

—Robert Frost

Why did I spend more than thirty years logging endless miles on highways, interstates, unpaved back roads, and ancient mountains, searching for customers to buy cookies, cigarettes, food, novelties, and chemicals? The answer wandered ahead of me as I began to write about my road adventures.

My adolescence was all about adventure. Daddy took my brother, sister, and me fishing. We often spent weekends discovering hidden caves or exploring lakebeds in search of arrowheads. My sister, ten years younger than me, could not scramble through nearby woods with me. No girls my age lived in our Knoxville neighborhood, but we had scores of boys for playmates. When the boys built tree houses, dug for fishing worms, or climbed Sharp's Ridge, I became one of the guys. Any time a boy double-dog dared me, I accepted and usually won. A dare might require me to climb a tree, but sometimes the tree was so tall, I screamed for my brother.

"Sonny, help me!" He always rescued me when I couldn't climb down.

When a neighbor boy once dared me to eat poison ivy, I was willing. Mama snatched the plant from my hands right before it reached my mouth. She developed a serious reaction to the toxic oil. I didn't even get a rash.

Exceptional and adventurous women figure in my family story. Grandmother operated a neighborhood grocery store in Knoxville after Grandfather died, while also managing several rental properties. My mother worked in her mother's grocery as a child. When she grew into a teen, she drove to customers' homes in her grocery truck and wrote orders, delivering them the next day—daring for a young woman in the 1930s. Mama was a saleswoman before I ever entertained the idea. She kept a gun under her car seat in case trouble befell her or her groceries.

Mama kept me company on some far away trips I would later make alone. We stopped at a pawnshop in Harlan, Kentucky, where she bought me a pistol to keep in my car.

Great Aunt Muriel became the first director of nurses at Baptist Hospital in Knoxville. She traveled the world as an Army nurse who helped open a hospital in Ceylon (now Sri Lanka), where she lived for many years. I learned the equality of both sexes.

After I entered school, different treatment of males and females made little sense to me. Crossing guards were always boys. Girls did not even get to dust erasers outside—a chore I coveted. *Read with Dick and Jane* did not impress me because Jane wore frilly dresses when playing. My choice of apparel was jeans. Disappointment greeted me again in high school. Girls were required to learn home economics. I asked if I could select shop or auto mechanics instead. The principal offered cosmetology as a compromise. Some compromise.

Feminism via authors and champions for women's equality, Marilyn French and Betty Freidan, arrived too late for me. Now married with two children, I earned a small salary doing tedious office work. Working life seemed unfair for women. Employees referred to the men in charge as "Mister" while addressing office "girls" by their first names. This practice reminded me of chalkboard erasers and crossing guards.

My last office job for a milk broker in the late '60s provided a distressing routine. I diligently performed my duties after one of my bosses, Mr. White, told me, "I want you to familiarize yourself with our files." I spent workdays reading about boring milk prices. When the building custodian resigned, Walter White called me into his office.

"If you could stay over a half hour or so, I want you to empty wastebaskets. You could also run the vacuum and then dust my office." I silently seethed because he assumed the woman should clean the office.

Office work was not for me, and neither was custodial service. Defeated, I continued to search for a job that would allow some independence. The road that led me to outside sales covered tough terrain, basic training for what lay ahead.

Childhood adventures, family role models, and simmering anger toward patronizing bosses all played a part in my wandering roads. No matter the hurdles, I sought freedom and adventure. Then too, I felt I had been double-dog dared.

THE KNOXVILLE JOURNAL
Thursday, May 13, 1954

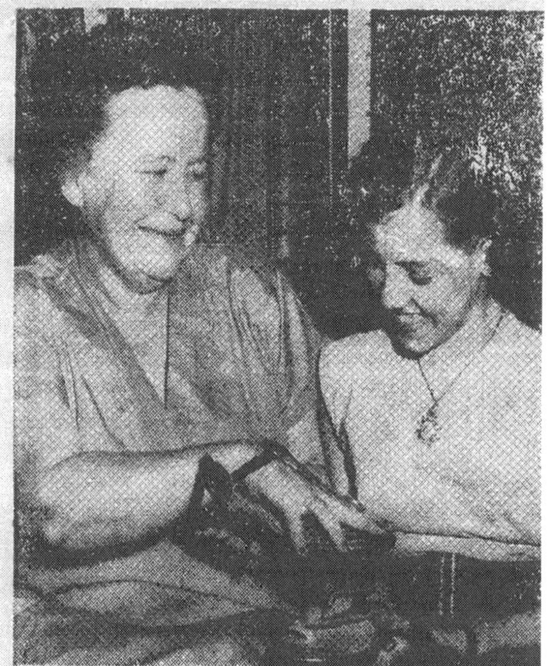

HEADS CEYLON NURSING SCHOOL—Miss Muriel Kragh (left), former supervisor of nurses at East Tennessee Baptist Hospital, is in Knoxville visiting her sister, Mrs. G. W. Spalding, 907 Chicamauga Avenue. Miss Kragh organized and is now principal of the Kandy, Ceylon School of Nursing. She works for the World Health Organization, an agency of the United Nations. Above, Miss Kragh shows her great niece, Diana Amann, 12, a pair of shoes—the type commonly worn in Ceylon. Diana is the daughter of Mr. and Mrs. Walter Amann of 706 Banks Street."

Great Aunt Muriel

Chapter 1
Culture Shock Waves

I was sitting in my cubicle today and I realized ever since I started working, every single day of my life has been worse than the day before it.

—Peter Gibbons, character in the 1999 movie *Office Space*

The Kingdom of Morocco became my home for five years. I married my second husband after he received orders from the Navy for American Embassy duty in Rabat, the capital. An ex-husband who still stalked me three years after we divorced had stolen my childhood self-confidence and adventurous spirit. My shrouded soul craved adventure, and Morocco felt like the right one.

I was excited about this journey to a fabled country; at twenty-eight years old, I would experience my first plane ride as well as my first venture out of our United States. Leaving office life and my ex-husband helped offset the sadness of goodbyes to family and friends. My husband, Wayne, my girls, Kelly and Cheryl—ages eight and seven—and I drove to JFK from Knoxville. We were on our way to Morocco.

The expected culture shock lasted less than a week. We lived "on the economy," which meant military families not stationed on the Naval base lived in Moroccan neighborhoods and shopped locally. A large number of families ate little more than canned food, purchased at Navy commissaries thirty miles away. They feared everything indigenous. I found my lost confidence, learning that simply attempting to speak local languages gave me independence and self-assurance.

I drove to market and ordered vegetables and meat in limited French or Arabic, rode a local bus, or hailed a *petit* taxi to Medinas, bargaining and joking with Moroccan merchants dressed in traditional Djellabas. I wanted to smell cumin and cilantro, drink mint tea, taste couscous and tajine, and relish all the beauty this magnificent land could offer.

My girls and I rode the Marrakesh Express several times, sitting among locals with their goats and chickens. We shopped for souvenirs, afterwards dining at diverse cafés. We became lost and found our way back to our train station. Each Fourth of July, we celebrated America's freedom with Moroccans, and citizens from many different countries.

We left Morocco only a few times during our tour, but never to return home to America.

Cheryl developed a medical condition that our Navy medic at Kenitra, Morocco, was unable to treat, so we flew to Rota, Spain, several times. Rota boasted a superior hospital at the naval base.

No one in our hospital dorm room would leave the security of the Navy base.

"Foreigners are scary," I overheard. "They kidnap Americans for their money."

Not in 1970s Spain were we in danger of being kidnapped. We possessed little money, but we forged ahead into intoxicating Rota. Cheryl and I took a local bus and ventured into town where we relished the cuisine of southwestern Spain. She and I found the subway and took our first subway ride. Another time, we traveled to Wiesbaden, Germany, to visit the medical facility in that picturesque country.

After Cheryl's hospital visit, we enjoyed few days of sightseeing. When we returned to Rabat, we realized the day was coming when we would soon have to leave North Africa. I believe they dragged me and drugged me to get me on our plane to return home. I didn't ever want to leave Morocco.

I experienced cultural shock after we returned to America, where my husband's next duty station was in Pensacola, Florida. Grocery stores didn't sell cumin. No one drank mint tea. No restaurant served couscous. People I met both socially and in the business world struck me as similar, with little variety in race or culture. Most folks lacked interest outside of their own small worlds. Burger King was *the place* to eat lunch. In 1975, no ethnic diversity populated any office I visited.

Enlisted Navy personnel didn't receive hefty salaries, so I looked for a job soon after we arrived. My last work experience had been as secretary at the Rabat-American Club in Morocco, a fun and exciting place to work. The boss didn't require us to punch time clocks, and he joined us as we drank during the daily happy hour. When the faint odor of hashish drifted through our office, we knew our Moroccan chef would serve his special brownies that made us all cheerful. While reminiscing about Morocco, I continued to look for a job in Pensacola.

The position I accepted in Pensacola, as liaison between "rack jobbers"

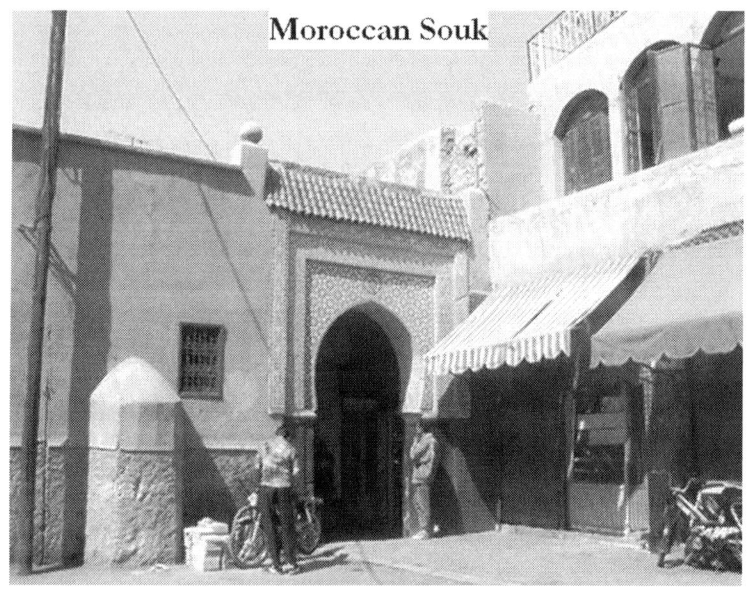
Moroccan Souk

(men who set up and wrote orders for light bulbs, toys, hardware, and hair care in convenience stores) was restricting and tiresome. I punched my first time clock but wanted to punch a live person. The idea of remaining in one building for nine hours appalled me, but office experience was all I had to offer any company.

Sometimes, I went with the guys in order to learn packaging, size, and cost of every product sold by our company. Being away from the office and visiting an unfamiliar town was pleasant. When one of the rack jobbers resigned, I pleaded with my boss, Mr. Bear.

"I know this route. I have learned the customers and products. Please let me take his route job!"

Mr. Bear scoffed, "We never hire women for these positions, honey. Route jobs are much too dangerous for ladies."

Outside sales was certainly not as dangerous as sitting in a smoke-filled office all day, I mused. I made appointments with our buyers, who were always men, on behalf of sales representatives from companies like G.E.,

Breck Shampoo, and Timex Watches. More women were beginning to have careers, and professional sales was a good fit for many of them. I admired those women with expensive suits and leather briefcases. Their companies provided company cars for them. A career in sales sounded easy: simply make an appointment with a buyer, take him to lunch, and leave a few product samples.

When my husband retired after three duty years in Pensacola, we moved home to Knoxville. I began my quest to land a position in sales, which I thought would be easy. I assumed my experience would be valuable to any company dealing in non-food grocery supplies. My first interview took place with a distributor of novelties advertising in my local newspaper. He wanted someone to handle customers similar to those Florida stores.

"Sweetheart, we have men waiting on these jobs," my interviewer reprimanded me.

Next stop—a business where the Man Who Hired scolded, "Ma'am, in Knoxville, women belong in offices, not outside sales." Navy retirement provided only a small salary, so I reluctantly accepted part-time work while searching for a sales position. Two contrasting offers arrived a few days apart.

A University of Tennessee employer offered me an office position that included excellent benefits. The day after I almost accepted UT's offer, a recruiter from a cookie company called me for a temporary route. Granted, no benefits were included, but I said yes to the company because it involved an outside position. I gleefully said goodbye to bossy Mr. Bosses.

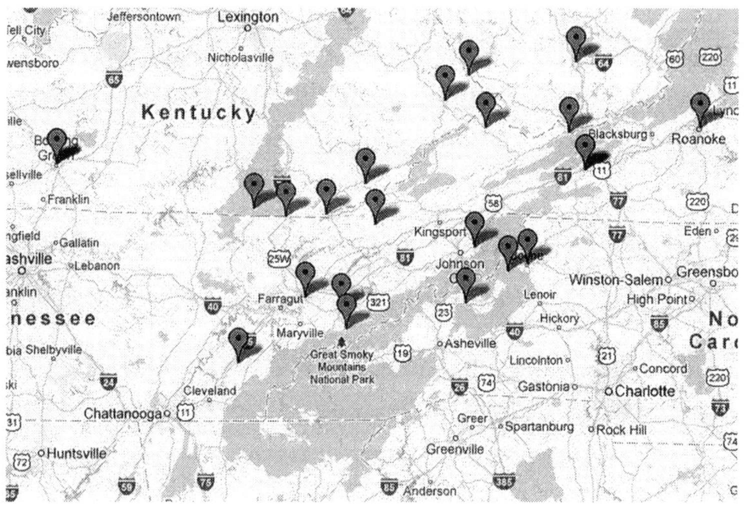

Sales Route - Cookies, and Snacks, and Racks, Oh My!

Chapter 2
Cookies and Snack and Racks, Oh My!

Selling cookies helped me to realize that you needed to have a certain way to communicate with people.

—Maria Bartiromo, American journalist and novelist

Selling Keebler cookies and crackers sounded like fun. I didn't know what the Keebler Elves wanted, until they told me.

"Your position will involve taking orders and refilling cookie shelves in grocery stores when a route person is on vacation." That sounded fine, except that I had foreseen accounts being located in Knoxville, instead of in towns like Williamson, West Virginia, Pikeville, Kentucky; or Jellico in East Tennessee.

How would I find my way to these remote accounts when my knowledge of Appalachia was limited to Knoxville and the Smoky Mountains? I had no idea what would ensue, so accepting the route job felt daring and even scary.

"Your company doesn't provide a vehicle for temporary employees?" I asked timidly.

"I'm sorry, you must use your own car," explained the interviewer apologetically.

"I'll be driving my own car, you say?"

My *own* car. My own car with no air conditioning. And it was summer. My own straight-shift car that would not go into reverse? My *demon* car without a radio or tape player? Well . . . yes.

A few days of working for Keebler brought awareness of the transformation surrounding Knoxville's borders. Driving twenty miles away from my city brought me to an abundance of craggy mountains, rural towns and hamlets, hills, and valleys. Magnificent scenery, isolation, and solitude comforted and thrilled me yet kept me uneasy on unfamiliar roads.

Driving my *own* car, I set out on a Fudge Stripe, Zesta Cracker, Chips Deluxe, and Pecan Sandies tour of southern Appalachia. The work was not difficult. Customers embodied pleasant small-town personalities, and everyone loved Keebler Snacks. UPCs (Universal Price Codes) weren't yet standard on grocery items, so my job required loading cases onto a cart, wheeling them into the store from a storage area, and then labeling the

packages of cookies and crackers with a pricing gun before placing them on store shelves.

In many older, messier stores, I brushed aside rat or mouse droppings before stocking shelves. I wore gloves and shuddered at the thought of assault by a rodent. Thankfully, nothing more than tiny, black specks appeared.

My job included unexpected advantages (I foolishly thought.) Spending a few nights away from home and my kids and sleeping in a pleasant hotel with room service would be idyllic. My daydream proved delusional. Hotels proved to be cheap motels. Room service was nonexistent. My first overnight stay found me at the only lodging in town—"Bates Motel," next to a raucous ABC Package Store. Survive the night I did, staying awake with a chair propped against my door and one light bulb stalking me from a drooping ceiling. The Keebler Company promised only temporary employment, so I continued sending applications elsewhere.

A promising phone call came from a novelty company that asked me to fly to Roanoke, Virginia, for an interview. Sure, wow! Yes, here came my dream job. MidEastern Distributors sent me a plane ticket. I flew to Roanoke, and they offered me a once-in-a lifetime position as representative for an area that had not been worked in months. After a week of training in Virginia, the company sent me home with a company car.

Well, not *exactly* a company car, but an elongated cargo van, loaded (by me) with cases of batteries, light bulbs, toys, and the always popular Goody Hair Care products. The manager packed maps, order books, and customer lists into my van. I had no confidence in handling this large vehicle that lacked a rearview mirror. *Goodbye and good luck; you are on your own.*

Okay, I could only hint at calling myself a salesperson instead of a deliverer and an order taker, but, hey, it was a step closer to my vision of becoming a genuine pharmaceutical rep or at least a representative for "The Jolly Green Giant." The company assigned me a traveling path with even more remote mountain hamlets than I had traveled with Keebler. I remained apprehensive over the possibilities of trekking into unknown land. But freedom of the road, distance from chauvinist bosses, and promises of an excellent future income kept driving me and kept me driving.

MidEastern Distributors' office manager, Katie, was a lovely young woman with good looks hindered by blond hair styled in a massive Afro. Katie's duties included mapping my territory each week. Traveling outside of Roanoke was not among her experiences, thus she lacked the ability to visualize distances between towns. Katie would stare at her office wall map, make a circle with her thumb and finger, and close one eye to ascertain my driving time from one customer to the next.

"Roanoke looks pretty close to Williamson, West Virginia," she would assume. "You should be able to load your van and drive to Williamson, then back to Knoxville today."

"Four hundred and eighteen miles, plus delivering and writing my orders in many accounts isn't possible in one day!" I protested. Sometimes, I spent the night in an unfamiliar little town, paying for my own motel. MidEastern Distributors refused to pay motel expenses if Katie insisted her plans were feasible. Fortunately, her district manager soon assumed route-planning responsibilities, and my itinerary edged toward sanity.

My new route took me to Ducktown, Dogtown, Turtletown, Deer

Lodge, Byrdstown, Bulls Gap, Pigeon Forge, Raccoon Valley, Elk Valley, Banner Elk, and all through the animal kingdom. Finding my way soon became easier, and I delighted in exploring varieties of Appalachian counties.

Time travel, I discovered, is not always science fiction. These small towns on my new route were places magically sent from my childhood of the '40s and '50s. IGA stores, locally owned banks, and hardware stores lined each downtown sidewalk. My first visit to Tinsley-Bible drugstore in Dandridge, TN, washed waves of nostalgia over me, and for a moment, I believed my age to be seven or eight.

Tinsley Bible Drugstore boasted a soda fountain resurrected via a time machine. The pharmacist who doubled as store clerk asked me to place toys not on racks, but in bins much like five-and-ten cent stores of the past. Next door, a friendly variety store owner fetched merchandise himself to fill customers' needs as he handed me a slip of paper with his handwritten order for batteries or light bulbs. I lingered longer than necessary because of enjoyable conservations with these two fine gentlemen about fishing and mountains and Appalachia.

The Moroccan spices I craved were not readily accessible in the '70s and'80s south. But a gourmet store in the quaint, artsy town of Banner Elk delivered a welcome discovery. Inside, I spotted cumin, opened the glass bottle, and orgasmically inhaled the potent spice's aroma. Then I reached for saffron...

Overnight stays again found me in Appalachian towns with few motels or eateries. Many people may not remember those days before cell phones, faxes, phone cards, or e-mails, but these *were* those days. Pay phones? Tricky to find one that worked. ATMs? Not yet in these areas. Charge cards for gas? Nope, never had one. Eating alone at night in a restaurant? *I must be looking for a man.*

Any evening I dared venture into a restaurant, a hostess would glance at me with a twinge of annoyance and icily inquire, "Can I help you?" On the other hand, she sweetly asked single men waiting for a table, "One for dinner?"

A female salesperson in small, Appalachian towns was often met with

Tinsley Bible Drugstore

suspicion. My work required me to haul display racks, load them into stores, price each item, and then fill the racks. Pulling into Grundy, Virginia, one day, I located my customer's drugstore and parked in front of a bank with large glass windows. First, I unloaded my handcart along with cases of products. Next, out came an unwieldy, metal rack. I struggled, dropped a few boxes, closed the van doors, and looked around to see the entire population of the bank and half of Grundy, noses pressed against windows, peering at me. I waved meekly and continued my battery and light bulb chores.

I was apprehensive about driving hundreds of miles in unknown territory, but I remained committed to gaining experience so that I might eventually join an exclusive, well-known corporation with a company car, designer

clothes, and fat salary. I had acquired acrophobia since my tree climbing days, and driving the Appalachian Mountains terrified me. In order to have some company on these trips, I invested in a Citizens Band radio. A CB would also keep my mind off the dizzying summits of Virginia and West Virginia mountains.

CB radios were not my field of expertise, so I hesitated before using one. I usually just listened, thinking that if van trouble arose, this CB would provide a way to get help. After a few trips over mountains to Williamson, I gathered my nerve and held the CB microphone, daring to talk to truckers whizzing by.

"Does anyone have the time?" I asked timidly.

In a couple of minutes, a gruff male voice answered, "Time for what, Darlin'?"

Over and out.

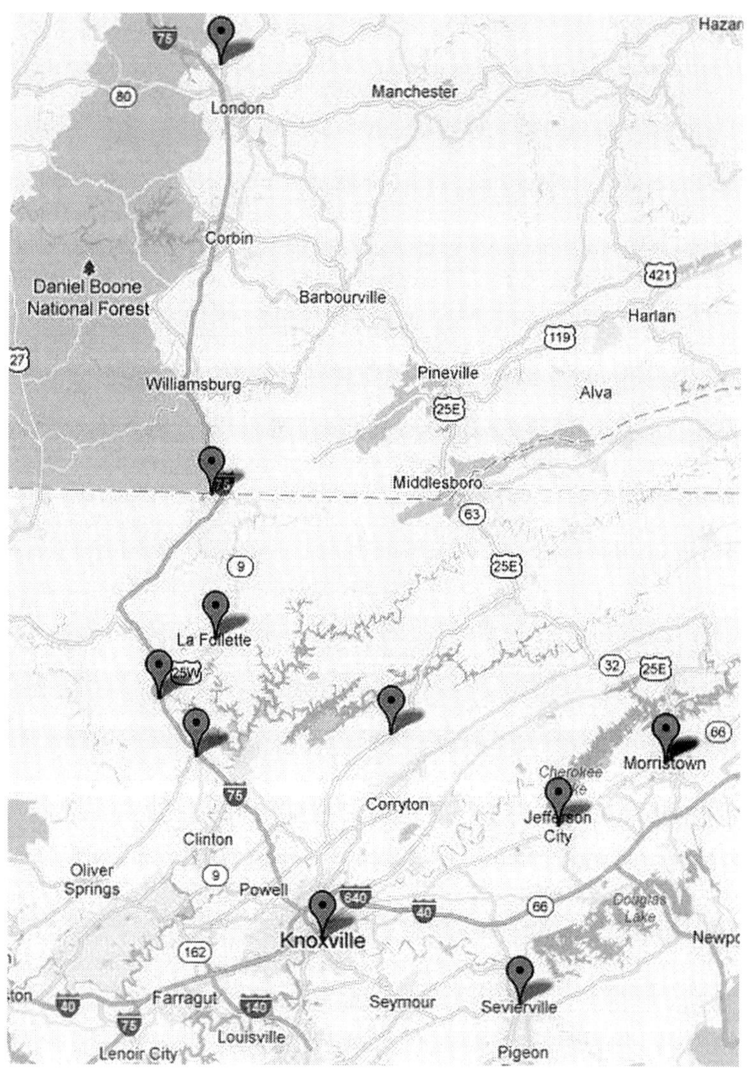

Sales Route - Over the Mountains and Lost in the Woods

Chapter 3
Over the Mountains and Lost in the Woods with Candy, Tobacco, and Restaurant Goods

Where was I going? I puzzled and wondered about it till I actually enjoyed the puzzlement and wondering.

—Carl Sandburg

I hold the world's record for getting lost. I've driven more than one of my vehicles through Cherokee Forest when I needed to be in Harlan, Kentucky. Signal Mountain atop Chattanooga? Not my friend, when my next appointment waited eighty miles away and down a mountain in Sweetwater, Tennessee.

Try to ask a local person where the drugstore is when you are lost in Big Stone Gap, Virginia. Citizens living in between small towns often think a stranger knows where the Jones' Barn stood before the fire because there is where you turn. Right is never right—it's "cut up." Left isn't left, but "cut back." You should learn these things before becoming lost in the country or the mountains. I found numerous accounts located at "20 Plumb Street" which is country for "twenty miles out and plumb up in the sticks."

I enjoyed merchandising drugstore racks, but this job ended sooner than I hoped. MidEastern Distributors closed after I worked for eight months. Next job search landed me at Tobacco Sales Company where they offered a territory in Knoxville and surrounding counties.

The business distributed tobacco, including cigarettes, chewing tobacco, candy, and novelties. The bosses instructed me to take orders from convenience stores. I also straightened and dusted their shelves and suggested novelties for the front counter.

I did not find the work difficult unless I forgot to order Pall Malls, Skoal chewing tobacco, or Hershey bars. Again, no company car. I bought an old station wagon and hauled as many open cases of cigarettes as possible in the event a business ran out of a favorite brand and our truck would not deliver for a few days. The car never lost that tobacco smell.

Junky items paid the highest commission, so in the tobacco job I learned the excitement of competition. My novelty commissions became the highest in the sales force. The buyer found many good selling items for us to promote, like the Pocket Fisherman. We pushed jewelry in little heart-shaped boxes, trick lighters, and fuzzy stuffed animals to make customers' children beg.

Many weekends, I loaded my car and drove through the same territory again. I'd been missing mountainous Appalachia. I stopped at every bait shop and Mom-and-Pop store until I sold out. Cash only. I would receive my commission after the staff counted the sales and subtracted cost of goods.

I sold hundreds of dollars in novelty items during my out-of-state trips, and I looked forward to the extra money.

The sales manager explained, "We can't afford the extra commission at this time because overall company profits are down."

"But my sales brought in extra money for you, and the commission is mine," I argued in vain.

My manger told me to wait a few weeks and, "We'll see."

The commission at Tobacco Sales didn't amount to much money anyway, especially since I didn't receive all they owed me. The work became monotonous except for my Appalachian trips. I drove to the same places, wrote the same orders weekly.

In addition, a tiny flicker of conscience rode with the cargo, whispering, "You are selling deadly tobacco." After three years, the little voice won. Time to look for something better. I didn't want to be simply an order taker, and I no longer cared to distribute cigarettes. By now I'd acquired enough experience, but my age hindered me from getting hired by a major manufacturer. I encountered only sales reps who appeared young, good looking, and unsullied by life on the road.

The next offer came from a restaurant supply company in London, Kentucky, seeking someone with experience to open a territory in East Tennessee. The catch? The distributor had *no* accounts in East Tennessee. I did get a company car, so I remained naïvely unconcerned with the absence of customers.

This distributor hired two other women for the Knoxville area and surrounding counties at the same time they hired me, and we were each assigned specific areas to work. After an extremely boring week of training in East Bernstadt, Kentucky, we learned the many varieties of green beans and pickled okra. Only one of the other women who'd been hired showed up at the training. I met my co-worker, Sarah, who was to become a lifelong friend. We laughed together about green beans, and we both confessed shock that the county in Kentucky was a dry one. Sara admitted she could survive the week if she only had a bottle of Scotch.

"I'll get us one," I vowed. I called my husband, Wayne, and explained our plight. Two hours later, he arrived with a most welcome bottle of Chivas Regal. Sara still talks about our special delivery that helped us through the green bean seminars.

When the week ended, I knew I must sell the groceries I learned about in Kentucky. Map in hand, I drove my company Camry through my territory, which included East and North Knoxville and several surrounding counties. I spent my days searching for restaurants, nursing homes, hospitals, jails, or any other location that served food.

Cold-calls intimidated me. In my last three jobs, customers had already been established, and my work only involved filling orders or delivering merchandise. This food sales position forced me to engage customers, introducing my company and me. I had a set route and could guess which businesses to contact. If food was involved, I made the visit.

The realization of what I faced set in as I found that large restaurants remained fiercely loyal to their present suppliers. A few small Mom-and-Pop diner owners explained, "We could use two dozen eggs and a case of French fries." Similar requests came often, but the modest quantity did not justify a delivery-truck stop. A new customer must meet a minimum order before the company would deliver to them.

Competition was fierce, especially since no female food-sales representatives had ever worked in East Tennessee. Local salesmen and prospective customers alike barked disapproval. Companies in Kentucky employed several saleswomen, so hiring us wouldn't have seemed unusual in that state. We tried to "open the Knoxville area" when the city hosted the 1982 World's Fair, but our competitors claimed we were there only for the fair and would abandon this territory as soon as it closed.

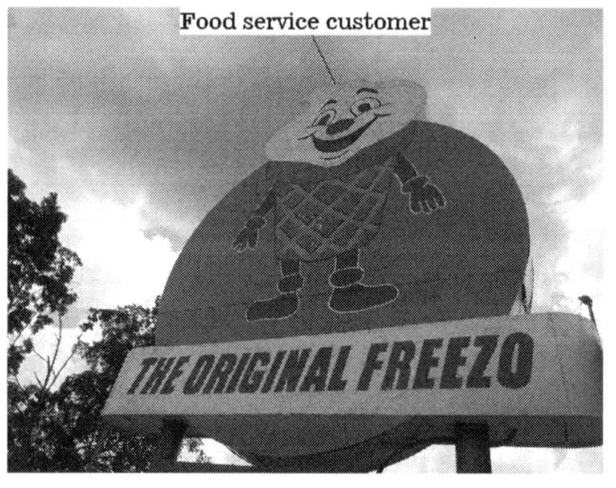

Food service customer

Often, I heard a food service buyer use the excuse, "You people are only here to get business from the World's Fair, and you'll leave us without a supplier when the fair is gone."

Or, worded slightly differently but with the same underlying message, "My food supplier told me not to purchase from your company—that you're only in town for fair business. Besides, women shouldn't be route salespeople."

An infamous buffet restaurant that served all-you-can-eat food in a trough, er, on buffet tables, refused to hear about my prices and service, a manager telling me, "I can't imagine how a female could know anything about selling food!" No, absolutely not. Women know nothing about food.

No one from the company in Kentucky ever sold any food at the World's Fair, but the distributor is still competitive in the Knoxville area.

Tough customers, especially restaurants, purchased mainly based on price. Some county school lunchroom managers could buy from whomever they wanted, and I picked up many of those accounts. Country restaurant owners cared about quality, delivery schedules, and low costs. Chain restaurants were out of the equation because corporate office purchasing agents handled food contracts. Frustrated and wanting to give up this customer search, I realized the only way I could find large accounts was to seek food service business in areas where my competition was not selling.

Norris Dam

Camp Tanasi, near Norris, Tennessee, and hidden away by Norris Lake, required a tremendous amount of food for Girl Scout troops who camped with them. I stumbled on this scenic lodging by accident as I drove around Norris State Park, searching for eateries. Camp Tanasi had been buying from only one vendor for the past few years but wanted to compare prices with other suppliers. No other company had bothered to answer their requests for service. When I gave them my food prices, the buyer, Stephanie, was astonished.

"We've been paying more than *triple* your prices for food according to your price list, and the other company delivers only once a month. If you come see us every week, I promise you all the camp's business." My company agreed to deliver twice weekly because Stephanie's supply orders amounted to a large account. She became a friend as well as one of my best customers. I kept this account as long as I worked for the food distributor.

Knoxville Job Corp, now defunct, surprised me as another large account. No food company was sending a sales rep to see them; they placed orders by phone. The college's facility manager, Hal, a big, burly African American with an enormous Afro (it *was the* 1980s,) appeared shocked at our prices.

"No supplier has sent anyone to call on us, and we require a tremendous amount of food each week. Diana, you have my business. I'll also give you the name of Knoxville College's Food Service buyer, and I'll call him for you." Knoxville College was located on the same grounds as the Knoxville Job Corp.

Hal kept his word. Job Corp turned into an extremely profitable account, both for me and my company. Knoxville College, a historical black college founded in 1875, purchased from me for several years and even continued to do so later when I worked for a different company.

I had acquired two healthy businesses, but the search was on for still more customers. Each account was unique. Learning a multitude of buying practices kept me busy.

Food supervisors' buying practices for healthcare facilities were daunting. I was shocked when Brenda, kitchen manager for a large nursing home, confessed, "We are only allowed to spend eighty-nine cents on food per patient per day." Subsequently, the food they purchased looked and smelled unappetizing. The odor of beef and broccoli swirled together in a blender wrecked my appetite for the rest of the day. I seldom saw fresh vegetables or fruits. Mystery meat arrived frozen before cooks reheated it or swirled it in a blender together with spinach or peas. Without exception, my nursing home customers struggled to stay within budget, and I knew them to be caring, hardworking folks.

It Will Be A Great Day When School Lunchrooms Have All The Money They Need And The Air Force Has To Have A Bake Sale To Raise Money, read the poster in a school nutrition supervisor's office. School lunchroom managers were not responsible for menus. Government bureaucrats designed them. Cooks often planned menus around commodities they expected each month. Health inspectors popped in without notice. Auditors selected a school at random, and managers had to account for every penny.

During Reagan's administration, the federal government insisted that school cafeteria cooks count catsup as a vegetable and tally the number of French fries each child received. Somebody in Congress, with an extravagant salary and plenty to eat, decided twelve fries would be just about enough.

Entering the back door of any given restaurant, I observed what the general eating public never sees. One cafeteria, located in a shopping center, served disgusting food. Employees scouted nearby grocery store alleys for food placed in trashcans. They used the discards in the cafeteria. For example, cooks added cauliflower and potatoes past their prime to ground beef in order to stretch meat budgets. On one particular call, I observed a cook, cigarette dangling from his lips, allowing ashes to fall into uncooked meatloaf.

In addition, some eateries used appalling cleaning methods. Cooks poured sulfuric acid drain opener on floors, rinsed them, and then dumped the toxic mess outside by their dumpsters. Where were the health inspectors? I know—pestering school lunch ladies.

A majority of the buyers I located served decent food and expressed concern for their diners. I didn't forget these folks, and they became customers when I later joined another company.

A variety of restaurant owners and cooks kept me entertained along my route. I delighted in visiting two separate restaurants owned by two Greek brothers. Customers told me a story of an unforgivable argument resulting in one sibling leaving the restaurant and starting his own place—next door. Each brother would question me about orders I received from his sibling, trying to determine who had better revenue. I never told, but they continued to ask me anyway.

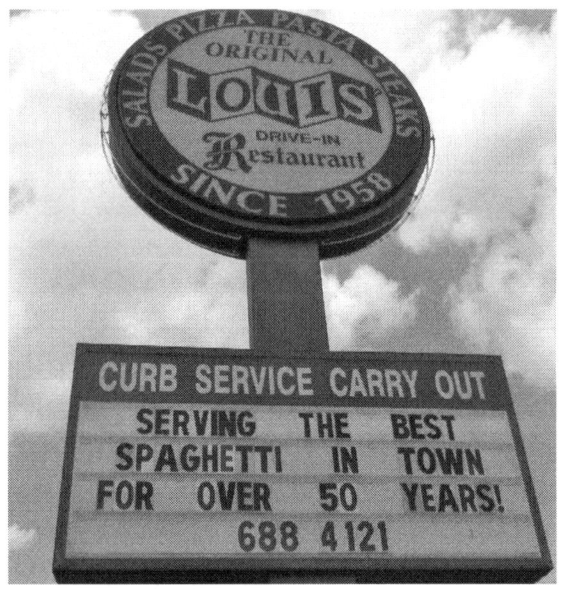

One pizza place ordered frozen pizza crusts and canned pizza sauce and secured a promise from me not to tell. Locally owned restaurants were most reluctant to buy from my company because we didn't carry White Lily flour and Crystal shortening in five-gallon buckets.

"Do you sell Chreeshtul? We can't make biscuits or cornbread without it. White Lily flour is the only flour we can use for cakes and biscuits." It was not an easy task to convince our purchasing agents that only these two products worked in Tennessee recipes. After all, people did make biscuits in other states. The company in Kentucky where I worked relented and brought in White Lily flour and Crystal shortening for us to sell. My sales volume improved.

A Mexican restaurant chain wanted only the lowest prices on cheese, so, twice a week, food service managers asked each rep to stop by with cheese costs. It seemed peculiar to me that a small, cost-per-pound difference could make a buyer drop loyal suppliers but pick them up again a couple of days later for half a cent.

Mr. Lee, a Chinese gentleman and one of my favorite customers, operated a small Asian restaurant in a shopping mall. He called me Diran, finding Diana tricky to pronounce. My name stuck, and everyone in my company began calling me Diran. One morning, Mr. Lee phoned me to request a case of red paper. Knowing we sold place mats, I keyed in an order for a case of them. Mr. Lee complained about his several hundred red place mats; he had wanted *red pepper*.

My job remained a route position and a mundane one: the same people, a monthly sales meeting in London, Kentucky, and an established territory that never changed. I missed the power of choosing which direction my car and I wanted to travel each day. I missed the mountains and valleys of Appalachia.

Despite my misgivings, I probably would have stayed with the food company had company policies not changed. Sales management hired new sales reps for all territories, and those reps then received half of our accounts. The company lowered commissions for all salespeople.

My boss rewarded my efforts by saying, "You've done a good job of getting new customers, and now we expect you to find a few dozen more."

I answered a few sales ads but didn't anticipate many offers. The new position I accepted turned out to be more difficult than I could have possibly imagined.

Lost in the woods

Selling Chemicals, Cold Call, Bold Calls, Old Calls

Chapter 4
Selling Chemicals: Cold-Calls, Bold Calls, Old Calls

The basis of optimism is sheer terror.

—Oscar Wilde

A plastic-haired, blue-polyester-suited, gold-chain-wearing, Monty Hall clone from Atlanta interviewed me in his hotel room at an Alcoa motel. The setting felt uncomfortable to me, and I wondered, why not conduct his interview in a coffee shop? Monty (his name actually was Monty) assured me, "My salespeople earn over $100,000 a year. They build swimming pools and drive Cadillacs."

I sensed that he overstated the possibilities, but I wanted a new job, and his offer of all of East Tennessee and parts of Kentucky and Virginia sounded intriguing, so I signed on.

To keep this job, my manager explained that I must sell three orders in five days or be dismissed. He declined to tell me that he had also hired several other people for my territory. Selling chemicals is one of the most competitive fields in this country. About one out of every ten chemical salespeople lasts only a month or so; therefore, the more hires, the better the chance that someone will *stick.*

For my first few weeks of chemical sales, training was non-existent. Office staff shipped me a six-pound catalog, three cases of chemicals, and an enormous, hard-sided sample case. Luggage wheels were not yet available on many cases, so I carried the heavy container into accounts until calluses formed on both hands. The company charged these materials against future commission checks. As I examined my chemical samples, I remained perplexed.

Janitorial supplies had been part of the food distributor's line, and Monty spoke as if I would be selling those familiar products, but this six-pound catalog contained hundreds of unfamiliar compounds. Chemicals ranged from air conditioning algaecide to zinc coating, from herbicides to insecticides, and included lubricants and disinfectants. How would I acquire five orders when my lack of understanding of these foreign products made selling them unrealistic?

Fortunately I had an advantage with my old food service customers, who came to my rescue and ordered chemicals suitable for kitchens. Five orders in five days allowed me to keep my job, and, in about a month, most of the other reps hired at the same time I was grew discouraged and resigned. Customers would continue to help me for twenty-six more years. They taught me products, gave me leads, and saved me orders

However, those few accounts couldn't continue to pay for my time and gas. My company provided a $350 weekly draw, money to help cover my expenses until I established customers. But considering charges for materials to help me sell, my commission statement remained in the red. In less than a month, my food customers had ordered their limits—I *must* make cold-calls.

Although my sales experience had been with three different companies, cold-calling had been limited to the food route and novelties I sold while employed by Tobacco Sales Company. When I entered kitchens of food service facilities—grocery samples and brochures from Kraft Foods, Tyson Chicken, or Smuckers in hand—buyers knew why I was in their office. Speaking to one individual at a time didn't intimidate me, as eateries had employed only one purchaser.

My first genuine cold-calls selling chemicals proved that layers of employees would be involved before reaching buyers—school secretaries, plant managers, purchasing agents, receptionists, and even garage mechanics with puzzled faces intercepted me.

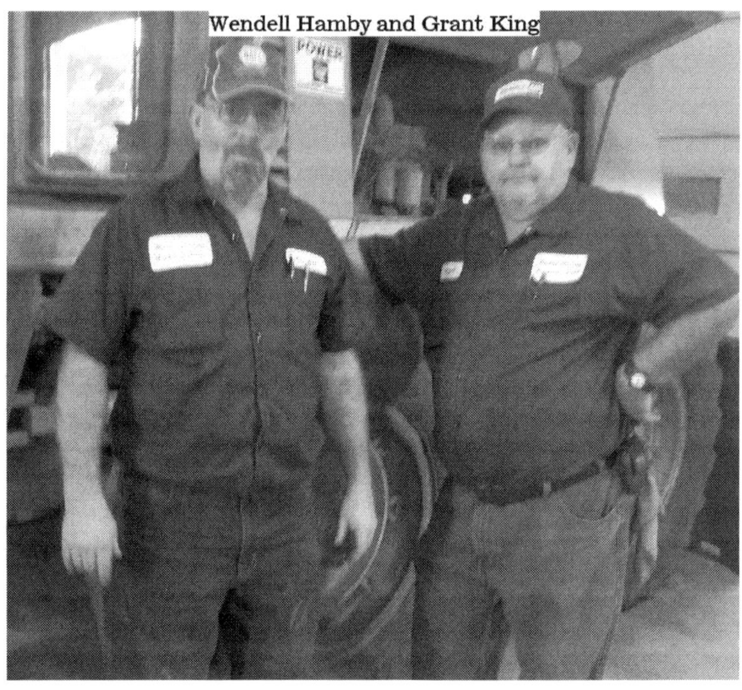
Wendell Hamby and Grant King

"Why is this woman in fancy duds in our greasy garage?"

These men had probably never encountered a female sales rep in their workplace. I wore a blazer over my outfits in the 1980s, summer or winter, as was the style. At least once a week, in hot weather, a garage employee would ask, "Whatcha doing with that coat on? It's too hot fer ya to dress like 'at."

Or sometimes, when I carried my briefcase into a garage, I would hear, "Why y'all carryin' such a big 'ol purse?"

Intimidation, hesitation, and trepidation kept me sitting in parking lots for hours, knowing I *must* go inside and find a buyer. I had no plans to crack the glass ceiling. I only wanted to break the sliding-glass window in front of the receptionist's desk. She, the Pekinese protector of bosses, robotically repeated, "He/she is busy. Leave your card."

My tongue developed bruises when so many new calls began with the person in charge bragging, "I'll just tell you how I buy my products. I try to get the best products at the cheapest prices." *What a brilliant concept!* I wanted to say, but I bit my tongue a thousand times instead.

Determined to learn the art of selling and lose my fear, I purchased every sales book and cassette available. When the renowned Zig Zigler brought his seminar to Knoxville, I purchased a costly ticket and attended with hopes of learning this motivational master's techniques. In Zig's first statement, he moaned that women had started entering the outside sales forces. He believed women should remain inside, working in offices, or, better yet, just stay home. Zig failed to motivate me.

Toastmasters would surely boost my confidence, so I joined the women's auxiliary, the Toastmistresses. Six boring and unbeneficial meetings later, no mysterious formula for successful cold-calls came to me. But help would soon arrive.

In a few weeks, Soapy Sales, district sales manager, came to ride with me and train me in his proven techniques. A pudgy, fast-talking young man, he presented his steps designed to make a sale:

1. Warm-up—hand the prospect a token gift, like a notepad, screwdriver, or pen.

2. Promote—offer the buyer an incentive, like a pocketknife or an item from our gift catalog.

3. Demo—show how a product works–spray a cleaner on the carpet or burn our grease using a trowel or torch. (One bizarre demo involved placing a beaker on a school principal's desk, adding a clean sanitary napkin and cigarette butts, followed by sulfuric acid. Thus, we demonstrated the power of our magic drain opener. Only once did I perform this exhibition. School offices filled with lung-choking black smoke and secretaries evacuated the building.)

4. Close—one could write a graduate thesis on closing techniques. I

vowed to learn as many as possible.

Additional sales managers came to work with me and showed me that my idea of cold-calling was not the way to find a buyer. Upon entering a company's front door, I had been asking to visit a purchasing agent, who then demanded, "Leave your brochure and prices. We will call you if we need anything." I waited for orders that never arrived.

In the years before our country's tragedy of September 11, 2001, customers rarely locked their side and back doors. Two salespeople walking uninvited into a wastewater treatment plant, a healthcare custodian's office, or an industry's maintenance department did not appear unusual, though management did frown on this approach. Sales managers taught me to find a back door or loading dock, give a cigarette lighter to the gate guard, and bypass the purchasing agent, along with other bold tricks to find my way into almost any account.

Wastewater treatment plant

My search for customers became bolder as I learned to carry a clipboard, and thus no one questioned my right to be in a building. By simply joking, and handing out logo pens, screwdrivers, or candy to employees, I could slip into almost any office.

Employees frequently asked me to leave; the rejections traumatized me. Tears barely waited to fall until I could see my car in the parking lot. Stubbornly, I persisted, winning sales contests and recognition in our company newsletter. Acknowledgment and the thrill of the close became a reason to spend many hours driving, stopping at twelve to fifteen workplaces each day.

A memory and emotion I had been chasing most of my life began to surface. In my school years of the '40s and '50s, educators cautioned parents against teaching children to read before starting school, lest they teach them incorrectly. It seems they also warned them not to compliment children, because my parents offered no praise for work well done. The first time I could *read my name* on the blackboard for the highest grade in class remains a thrill never forgotten. When I saw my name in my company's paper for top sales, I finally caught that elusive early memory.

Chemical selling started to become less terrifying and more satisfying, although the knowledge that no one on earth knew where I was most of the day remained both exhilarating and unnerving.

I felt concern for my children at home, teenager daughters Kelly and Cheryl, who often cared for their young brother, Brandon. Both sets of grandparents were nearby if an emergency arose. Luckily, none did. I drove happily along winding roads and over Appalachian Mountains.

Two years after accepting the chemical sales position, I began to cover my draw and receive a commission check each month. Customers, reluctant to buy because most chemicals sales reps stopped by one time, never to be seen again, ordered often from me. I became skilled at finding:

- School lunchrooms: look for mops on a loading dock
- Custodian's offices: find a cleaning cart
- Maintenance supervisors: follow a man holding a grease gun
- County highway departments: dump trucks sit outside the office.

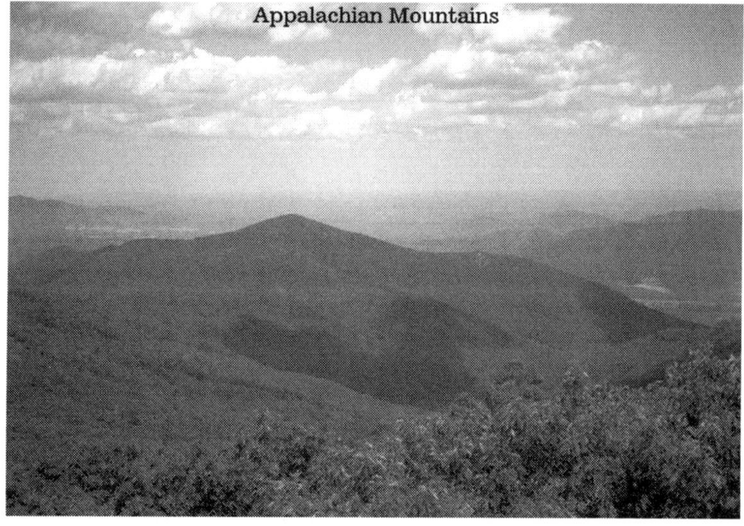
Appalachian Mountains

- Landfills: drive to the top of a hill filled with dirt, rocks, and waste

Landfill, Newport, TN

After three years in chemicals sales, I discovered coal mines. Ignoring my fear of heights, I drove up winding and twisting mountain roads overlooking deep ravines. These narrow roads with no guardrails kept me dodging huge, black dump trucks while searching for miners with purchasing power. Petros, Tennessee, and Eastern Kentucky were dotted with mines I visited when selling grease and hand cleaners. Coal miners gave the impression that they were alarmed at a woman with a sample case driving atop a mountain and looking for business, but I encountered welcoming buyers who seemed happy to see a visitor.

Undaunted, I boldly entered accounts, and I bluffed my way to a buyer's office, room, or toolshed. No customer in my territory was left unturned. I walked brazenly into sewage treatment plants, climbed down stairs to boiler rooms, entered back doors of industrial plants, or drove straight up bumpy dirt roads to ferret out rock crushers. I had no plans to climb the corporate ladder, but I *did* want to climb to the building's rooftop to find air conditioning units, sometimes called cooling towers.

My self-assurance improved. Customers became my friends, counting on me to show them the latest products while secretly hoping to receive a gift of a Case knife or perhaps donuts and a ball cap. I loved those now-familiar calls but still dreaded making cold-calls, though I could not rely on regular customers if I wanted to earn more income.

I started my day with two new calls, followed by dependable customers. After five years, new clients became loyal customers and produced a decent income for me. Cold-calls continued to start my day and kept me looking for new adventures on the road.

Even though selling chemicals remained challenging, I loved to trek anywhere through rainbows on the road: Brownsville, Bowling Green, Greenback, Greeneville, White Pine, Copper Hill, Red Bank, Bluefield, or Gray. Years before, these small towns lay but one Walmart away from the next, each one unique with Mom and Pop cafés, family-owned hardware stores, service station men who filled your gas tank, and customers who could purchase what they needed without giving their firstborn to a purchasing agent.

Locating accounts by using back roads and short cuts, making back-door calls, and learning to close the sale were not all the strategies I needed to sell chemicals. My knowledge of chemical products was extremely important if I wanted to obtain orders.

I, who didn't pass high school chemistry, learned the difference between a phenolic and a quaternary disinfectant, decided whether lithium or molybdenum lubricant should be used for a certain piece of equipment, and studied why climbing gear oil is important. I used an eggbeater to demonstrate the climbing characteristics of our gear grease. Engineers explained whether their machinery required 80- or 140-weight oil. Did the customer's weeds need a soil sterilant or broadleaf killer? What percent of solids did the hospital want in a floor finish (wax)? The pH of a cleaner often became a selling point—would neutral or acid work best?

Before offering gloves to them, I asked whether wastewater employees required vinyl, latex, nitrile, or powdered, as well as what length. Prices on air conditioning algaecide tablets depended on tonnage of equipment. Did grease buildup or roots cause stoppage in a pipeline? Would an enzyme work better than a d-limonene degreaser or perhaps a root killer? I became the person to call when my customers encountered drain problems, and I earned the title "Drain Surgeon."

Gaining product knowledge continued to be crucial. Solving a customer's problems rewarded me with fulfillment. When I demonstrated and sold the right lube, the mechanics proudly told me that the kingpins on their school buses lasted much longer. My hard work became worthwhile. I felt excited to find a cleaner that changed the grout in tiled kitchen floors from dirty gray to white. When I sold a floating lift station cleaner to the utility company, they told me that it controlled their grease situation. School bus maintenance men often ordered RTV silicone, and I helped them choose between red, white, clear, or black.

Of course, I admit that more than a few of my demonstrations turned into misfortunes. Citrus-based degreasers that kitchens purchased to dissolve grease and fat melted cooks' rubbery soles as they mopped the floors. Some of our grout cleaners, I discovered too late, turned floor grout white only because the acid product ate away the top layer of grout. After apologizing to customers, I printed instructions for correcting these problems. None of my sales managers had warned me of these potential risks.

Boilers in many small schools, churches, and hospitals were aged and badly in need of repair, but when replacing one would be cost prohibitive,

I learned to test boiler water and recommend treatment. Problems sometimes arose after the chemical treatment because old, built-up scale in the boiler tubes was all that held the fragile, rusty pipes together. After a customer explained this potential problem, I never sold boiler treatments unless I explained that pipes could possibly leak afterward. Any manager who ever rode with me tried to sell the treatment, no matter the risk. I thwarted the sale whenever possible.

In my first three years selling chemicals, I began to doubt the sales manager's routines, realizing they manipulated the people who paid our wages. I valued each customer. My philosophy of selling began to diverge from that of the company. The supervisory team hired to train reps did not concern themselves with customers receiving the correct product—they only wanted to "sell 'em anything."

During my fourth year in chemicals, I became a sales manager. I wanted to share with the new hires the attitudes I'd developed by taking the best that my managers taught while also recognizing that customers must be treasured and respected.

Chapter 5
Mishaps and Mayhem

We'll just have to get along. That's what people do, you know? They just get along. And try to help each other.

—Stephen King, *Cujo*

Mishaps and mayhem chased me during my day as I strove to be the top salesperson and win trips to exotic countries. Floor care products played a part in my sales as I eagerly demonstrated floor finish and stripper.

My first experience with a commercial buffing machine could have caused serious injury. An amazing new product, designed to eliminate the need for repeated stripping and waxing of tile surfaces, would be my best seller, I reasoned. My first call with this chemical was to one of Knoxville's hospitals. Gene, the custodian, let me demonstrate the phenomenal invention.

Gene brought his buffing machine into the hallway, and I poured a small amount of the new chemical onto the floor. How hard could buffing be? He turned on the machine as I grabbed the handles, anxious to shine the floors. Suddenly, the 1500-rpm monster spun down the hallway with me holding on for dear life. I couldn't let go until it finally slung me against a wall. I was bruised and particularly embarrassed because I'd told Gene,

"Don't worry. I know how to operate a buffer."

One snowy and icy day, an East Tennessee town about twenty-five miles from the Kentucky line loomed as my destination. Wartburg was deserted because of inclement weather. Even Mildred's Diner, "Home of the Famous Wartburger," remained closed. I should have stayed home. I pulled into a government housing development certain the manager would order ice melt. *Damn it.* My car was stuck in the snow. This incident happened long before the availability of cell phones. My only option seemed to be to walk to a unit in the development and ask for help. As I slowly opened the car door, I heard a growl. Peering out the window, I saw a menacing dog snarling and daring me to get out of the car. Wheels spinning, my car wouldn't move. Neither would Cujo. I rolled down the window partway and screamed for help. No answer came from a human, but the dog hurled itself against the glass in reply.

After what felt like hours, a pickup truck rolled into the driveway next to me.

"C'mere, Spike," the man, dressed in a utility company uniform, called to my little friend.

Spike followed his master, and I yelled for help! The friendly man pushed my car out of its snow bed, and then scolded me.

"Why are you out here on a day like this? Can't you see Wartburg is deserted?"

I waved goodbye to Spike and slid home without an order for chemicals.

My next snow adventure took place at Knoxville College.

Foolishly, I decided to track down a willing buyer on an unusually heavy snow day. My old customer, Knoxville College, surely needed snow-melting compound. Once again, my tires began spinning, and I became stuck in a snow-covered ditch.

Too late, I realized the college had closed for a snow day. I saw no one about to assist. I tried rocking the car, and then suddenly, like magic, several uniformed players from the college football team appeared. These large young men literally lifted my car out of the ditch and set it back on the road.

A giant linebacker cautioned me, "Ma'am, it's too dangerous for you to

be driving in a snowstorm. Please be careful going home. Do you want one of us to drive you there?"

"Thank you guys for your help. I'll be fine," I said, not wanting to ask them for anything else. I skidded home without a chemical order.

Product demonstrations often led to disasters since I never refused a customer's request and wanted to help each one no matter the problem. I also wanted a sale.

In the '80s and '90s, women in sales or offices wore business apparel. Dresses or skirts (lingering memories of grammar and high school) were the style, along with pantyhose and pumps. On days that didn't involve cooling towers, boilers, or garages, I dressed like a businesswoman, though I normally wore pantsuits. I ruined more than a couple of outfits.

One disaster involved sulfuric acid drain opener, a hazardous product. A customer telephoned one morning as I was leaving the office, wearing a blouse and skirt with the obligatory pantyhose. Skirts were an unusual choice for me, but this day I had on a new one.

"Diana, if you have a drain opener sample, please come to the church," pleaded Walter, custodian of a church in Knoxville. "And hurry! Our men's room floor drain is stopped up, and water's standing on the floor. The odor is disgusting. We're having Men's Prayer Group, and I have to clean up this mess."

I arrived at his office in half an hour. Walter walked with me to the men's restroom, and I confidently poured a small amount of drain opener into the floor drain. The caustic acid splashed, and, while maintenance employees watched, my pantyhose shredded, the legs fell off, and blisters covered my legs wherever the acid touched. I heard a great sucking sound, which assured me the drains were open, regardless of my mistake. I *knew* never to pour drain opener into standing water, but I had too hastily tried to solve the custodian's problem. Walter, a retired military officer and a kind, caring man, ordered several cases of drain opener from me anyway. I believe he just felt sorry for me.

One of my managers told me of a demonstration guaranteed to end with a sale. Brass plates adorned rental post-office boxes in the '80s. Soapy explained the demo this way: "These brass plates tarnish. They turn nearly black, and postmasters constantly seek a safe and effective cleaner to brighten them. Take our product, which safely replaces muriatic acid, to any post office. You should ask the postmaster if you may clean a few post-office boxes. He'll be amazed! Then sell him a drum of our cleaner."

So I stopped at our downtown Knoxville Post Office, where a postal clerk sent me to the head custodian, Mr. Wells. Confidently, I opened my sample case and took out a rag and my wondrous cleaner. Sure enough, the brass polished beautifully. As I grabbed my order pad, Mr. Wells, although impressed, hesitated.

"Come back here tomorrow, and let's see how the boxes look before I place an order with you."

No, no, no, I did not want to return. My product worked. He should sign my order form now! Reluctantly, I waited until the next day, expecting a large order and imagining all the post offices in three or four states buying from me.

"Come over here and look at our boxes," Mr. Wells instructed. The brass plates that I cleaned the day before had turned an ugly green, which is what happens when acid mixes with brass! I cleaned off the green goo, did not get an order, and never sold that product again. Postmasters purchased many products from me over the years—just not anything to clean brass. And most post offices now have installed stainless steel post-office box doors instead of brass ones.

All new chemical sales reps received a booklet explaining various types of accounts and what product to show in them. Health care facilities, municipalities, small industries, schools, churches, day care facilities, even restaurants. I undertook the task of making at least one call on each manner of business.

Sevierville County Highway Department garage, next on my list, loomed before me—my current challenge. I had never been in one. I parked behind the building and walked into the gloomy, noisy work area. The highway superintendent, Hank, suddenly stood before me. Boyishly attractive, with a John Deere ball cap nearly covering his forehead, Hank drawled, "Hep ya?"

"I'm your new chemical salesperson, and this is my first call on a county highway," I whispered, trembling.

"Ya'll go on up to the quarry and see if Mr. Henry needs anything," he pointed to the top of a dirt road. I found the open pit mine and Mr. Henry, the quarry operator—an elderly gentleman with full grey beard—whose lips seeped snuff.

He walked with me to the trunk of my car where I showed him hand cleaner, penetrating oil, tube grease, safety solvent, and about eight other products. To each sample, he nodded his head and spit tobacco juice near my feet. Then he spoke.

"Well, you can send me everything you done shown me. I can use it all," I gave him a ball cap and pocketknife and breathlessly rushed down the hill to write my order, which amounted to several hundred dollars. In the days before purchase orders became common, a verbal request sufficed.

Congratulations arrived from my manager via telephone message for my sizeable order. The next month, I returned to the highway department, hoping to place another order. Hank met me at my car with a scowl and arms folded across his chest.

"We have been the target of chemical salesmen's scams before, but you looked honest to me. You got Mr. Henry in trouble. Defend this $800 bill."

I attempted to explain that the products had been ordered, but he sent me back to the quarry to confront Mr. Henry.

"Honey, I only wanted one each of your chemicals, not a dozen." *My mistake.* In assuming he knew that one of each meant a case of twelve, and greedily writing his order, I had failed to make certain of the customer's needs. The superintendent kept a few cases and returned the rest to the company, "freight collect." My company deducted the freight charges from my commission. And after that experience, I listened carefully and asked questions when a customer said, "Send me one."

Sevierville, TN

Two incidents involving fuel remain embedded in my memory. In my traveling days, personal checks and cash reigned as methods to buy food or fuel. Years passed before I could rely on gas credit cards, so I had to fill up before trips more than a few miles from Knoxville. The day came when I forgot both gas and cash after my customer in Tazewell, Tennessee, requested a rush delivery.

Once I accomplished my Tazewell delivery, I headed to Middlesboro, Kentucky, to make a few cold-calls. As I approached Kentucky, my gas gauge empty light blinked. Unfortunately, my wallet was as empty as my head had been that morning.

With no phone booths in sight to call home for help, I panicked. "We do not accept checks," I heard at several service stations. Thinking I'd have to spend the night in my car, I spotted a Sears catalog outlet. I walked in and explained my situation while the kind salesman surveyed my tearful face.

"Against company policy, I will cash a check for $10. You seem honest, and if I lose my $10, I'll be surprised." The check didn't bounce.

I often felt as though I were in a state of frenzy. When cell phones finally became available, I depended on mine to stay in contact with customers. One day, I answered my cell phone while holding a fuel nozzle and pumping gas into my vehicle. The fuel hose jumped away from my distracted hand, pouring fuel on my clothes and the station driveway. As I tried to run into the station for assistance, I slipped in the greasy fuel, landed on my butt, and ruined yet another outfit.

Another mishap involved cooling tower and boiler treatment products. My company held a seminar on chemicals to remove sludge from boilers and clean roof top A/C and heating units. The company managers never mentioned potential disasters that could occur after marketing these products. A cleaner for the cooling towers required the use of an anti-foaming agent along with the caustic chemical. The next day after selling the product to a small county hospital, I received a frantic call from the hospital maintenance supervisor.

"Diana, you'd better get up here NOW! White foam is gushing from the rooftop and covering the parking lot and most of the vehicles."

I rushed to the hospital where chaos met me. In a panic, I phoned our company chemist, who admonished, "Didn't your manager tell you to sell a de-foamer with the cooling-tower treatment? We may have a lawsuit if any vehicles are damaged." Indeed, my manager had neglected to mention that important fact. Fortunately maintenance had diluted the cleaner correctly, and, after hosing the area, we found no harm to any car.

The best chance of making a sale proved to be by demonstrating a prod-

uct. Showing the customers how something worked often induced them to order the chemical for their business. One product I kept in my car was an aerosol grease that, when sprayed, emitted a black, tacky, molybdenum grease. My customer, Cocke County Highway Department, along the Tennessee-North Carolina border, usually purchased any new product I presented to them. The head mechanic just happened to need a clinging grease product for his asphalt pavers.

I pulled out my grease can, planning to spray a little on a trowel, when the can erupted. Black, extremely tacky grease soon covered my clothes, face, and glasses, as well as shooting onto the ceiling. My backfire amused the garage men, who laughed loudly. My clothes and glasses were ruined. The black gunk stayed on the ceiling for the many years that I visited this department. And the men always laughed when I walked into the garage.

My obsession with nice clothes caused more than a few mishaps, but the one I remember most concerned a dress marked way, way down in price. Certain I looked the saleswoman part, I proudly wore my new clothes two days in a row. Because we didn't visit buyers more than once a week, no one would see the outfit twice in one week. At the end of the second day, Mr. Mee, who whenever I arrived said, "Hi, I'm Mee," pulled at the back of my skirt and removed a price tag hanging halfway down my thigh. "K-Mart sure has some good sales. Your suit didn't cost very much." Yes, I had worn the K-Mart tag for two days.

The road offered still another environment for trouble. When at last I owned a cell phone, I often flew down the interstate while talking to customers and writing purchase orders. I learned to slow down after a couple of small accidents where I bumped into the rear of vehicles as I wrote orders while waiting for a red light to change. Fortunately, my mishaps never caused any significant injury.

Today, I'm a careful driver and realize my zealousness in pursuing business would never have justified causing a serious accident.

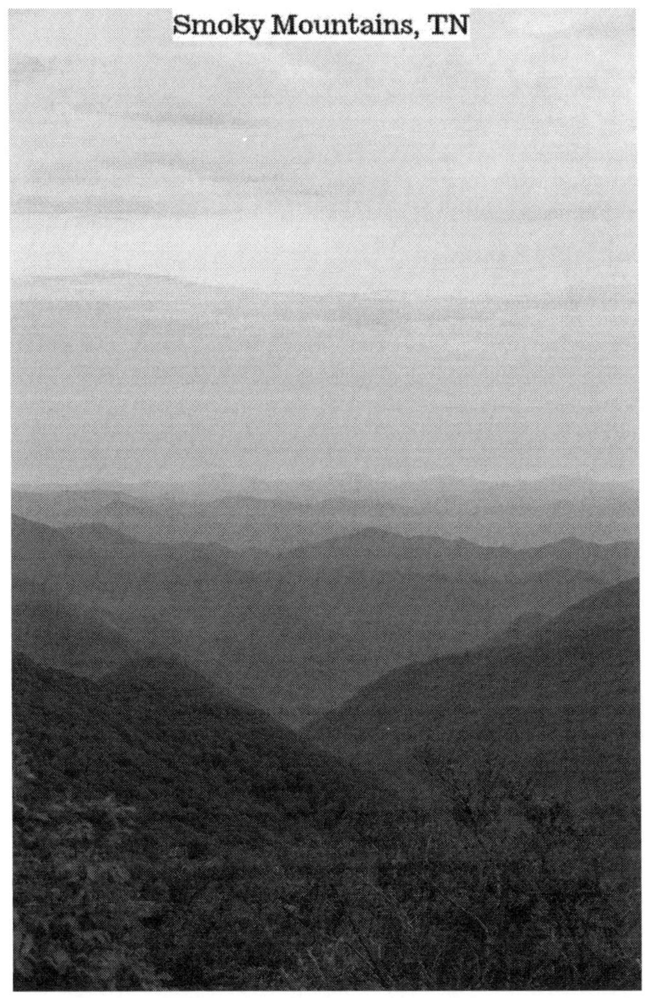
Smoky Mountains, TN

Chapter 6
Sales Manglers (Managers) and How They Mangle Their Sales Teams

(Names have been changed to better reflect the personalities of my sales managers.)

> *Most managers were trained to be the thing they most despise—bureaucrats.*
>
> —Alvin Toffler, American writer and futurist

Tazewell's entire tennis court, unevenly covered with foul-smelling, tar-like goo, had been resurfaced by a sales manager and me. Ben Dover, the gnomish manager/trainer up from Atlanta, wore bifocals with lenses thicker than windows on a Secret Service vehicle, and his New York accent was even thicker. Ben's manicured fingernails sparkled with clear nail polish, and he proudly looked at his hands every few minutes, except when the black slime oozed under his nails and into his toupee. I, covered in the same black gunk, felt embarrassed and terrified about the mess we made of the courts.

I then realized Ben was a deceptive salesman, living up to the reputation chemical sales reps and used car hawkers too often carry. Ben's tennis court incident is only one reason our sales force renamed managers "Manglers." Ben and his pushy salesmanship got us into this situation a few days earlier.

I'd been working for the chemical supply company for about a year when Ben Dover arrived to teach me his superior, New York City sales techniques. We made a call on the town hall in Tazewell, Tennessee, where we met the city manager. Tim Idly, a portly, pleasant man, resembled the child's toy called a Weeble. He welcomed both of us into his office, decorated with fishing paraphernalia and photographs of him holding his biggest catches.

"Fishing," he boasted, "is my life." He then told several tales of his many fishing trips to various Tennessee lakes.

Cove Lake, Campbell County, TN

At the end of his fishing stories, Idly announced proudly, "I don't buy no chemicals from them boys from Hotlanta."

"I live in Knoxville, not Atlanta," I assured him, but he remained adamant about his suspicions of salespeople up here from Georgia.

Mr. Dover tittuped to his car and magically produced a fancy, fish-filet knife decorated with our company logo. He presented it to the city manager. Mr. Idly then asked if we sold tennis court resurfacing paint. I hadn't yet learned about all of our products, but Mr. Dover answered, "Of course we do, and if you purchase from us, our company will do the resurfacing work."

Mr. Idly accompanied us to the green, badly worn town tennis court. My slick, double-talking trainer convinced the rookie official, "Green courts are no longer used, and we have an advanced coating system. Our crew can return within a week to give that old court a new look." We would indeed give it a "new look."

I had no inkling that crew meant Ben Dover and me. I hadn't signed up for manual labor. We arrived before dawn to begin our Augean task. As I naïvely read the labels on the miracle paint Ben had brought along, I questioned him.

"Why does the label say asphalt coating? Why are two long-handled paint rollers our only equipment?"

"No problem," he boasted. "I'll make this work." And work we did—from six a.m. until six p.m. in July heat on a sizzling surface. When the city manager arrived that evening to see his newly coated courts, plump tears fell from his cheeks onto the court and mingled with the sticky mess.

"You and your Hotlanta people have ruined my tennis court!" Well, we weren't both *Hotlanta* people, but yes, we had ruined it. Tim had authorized this purchase and would be in a difficult position with the city council because our venture cost the town several thousand dollars. We left him with the mess, and Ben Dover returned to Atlanta. The town of Tazewell sued my company, but I never learned any details. I tried to apologize to my former customer, but he refused to see me. I swore I would never work with Ben again, but my company insisted he was the Saint of Sales.

Our next excellent adventure involved Knoxville College, a good customer of mine. I dreaded taking Ben to this customer, but he insisted. I sold chemicals to many departments at the school, and I was afraid he would damage my relationship with my friends there. My apprehension turned out to be correct.

Ben Dover strutted into the college kitchen, where he approached twenty-year-old Rosita, a newly hired cafeteria manager. A pretty, petite African American, Rosita appeared to be shy and unsure of these unfamiliar vendors invading her cafeteria.

"Hi, Dear," Ben purred. "We have a promotion going on for kitchens only. Pick out a blender or toaster for yourself from our gift catalog, and I will send it to your home," he promised.* He then demonstrated a floor cleaner and wrote an order, which he pressed her into signing. The blender was charged against my commission.

I didn't understand exactly what chemicals he was sending her until I received an angry call from Knoxville College's purchasing agent.

"Why on earth have you billed us $2,500 for cleaning products? Come over here NOW and pick up this stuff. We don't want it." Wary, I drove to the school. Several items sat inside and outside the tiny kitchen: a 55-gallon drum of floor cleaner, a 35-gallon drum of oven cleaner, two 20-gallon barrels of insecticide, and an invoice for $2,500. Even though Rosita had signed for the sale, luckily Ben had failed to obtain a purchase order.

Knoxville College returned the products, and I was charged freight both to and from the college. Our company president chastised me for failing to obtain a purchase order; the trainer/manager had blamed me for the incident. Knoxville College accepted my apology and continued to purchase from me throughout my sales career.

On another occasion, Ben embarrassed a co-worker and me at a vendor's trade show. He had excitedly approached us both at a sales meeting, saying, "Good news! We are all three going to a trade show in Gatlinburg. We'll stay in a nice hotel and eat expensive dinners paid for by the company." Manufacturers and distributors of chemicals from all over the country, I learned, held yearly trade shows. Gatlinburg appealed to these suppliers since it was located in the scenic Smoky Mountains and prices were not as expensive as in larger, metropolitan cities.

Jane, our salesperson in Chattanooga, Tennessee, was thrilled at the mini-vacation, but I knew Ben too well. Suspicions floated through my brain.

*Gift giving for personal use was against company policy for municipalities, schools, or any government facility, although most salespeople skirted the rules by promoting the "gift" to be used for employee Christmas bonuses. Sometimes, a tool or kitchen gadget could be given to "Employee of the Month," or raffled at a company picnic, with proceeds going to charity or facility improvements. As far as I could determine, those managers who worked with me kept their promotions under the IRS limit:

IRS regulation 5 C.F.R. 2635, subpart B states: (a) Gifts of $20 or less. An employee may accept unsolicited gifts having an aggregate market value of $20 or less per source per occasion, provided that the aggregate market value of individual gifts received from any one person under the authority of this paragraph shall not exceed $50 in a calendar year.

How will he screw this up? He found a way.

We arrived in Gatlinburg and checked into our hotel rooms. We located the trade show, already in session, with booths filled with every type of chemical product imaginable. Customers milled about, holding bags to be filled with advertising gifts from each company representative.

As Jane and I looked for the booth and banner announcing our company, I knew I shouldn't ask, but I couldn't help it. "Ben, where is our booth? Did you UPS our products here already? I don't see our banner."

"Oh, that. I forgot to fill out the form and pay $150 for the booth. But we can have fun anyway."

Jane, Ben, and I walked around the conference area and checked out our competition. When several customers asked if we would be hosting a "hospitality room," I realized that each company provided drinks and food for them after the show ended. These happy-hour sessions took place in a chemical company manager's or owner's hotel room.

"Ben, we're supposed to host a hospitality room. We don't have any alcohol or food," I whined.

"No problem; you and Jane can go to the liquor and grocery stores. Get whatever we need. Buy a cooler and bag of ice, plastic cups, and we'll have a party."

Gatlinburg is dry, you dolt. And this town doesn't have even one grocery store. Jane and I drove to a gas station and bought beer and peanuts. (In Tennessee, beer is allowed in dry counties, but hard liquor is not. Go figure.) We didn't find a cooler, so we served warm beer and stale peanuts. Customers didn't spend much time in our party room, which was not a suite like our competitors rented, but a plain hotel room. People could choose to either stand up in the small space or sit on the bed. Another wasted opportunity because of a mangler.

Why did I stay with a company like this one? I was establishing good customers; I liked our products, and, unless a mangler rode with me, very few problems arose. Besides, I had signed a non-compete contract, and the fine print informed me that I couldn't sell any product from another company to any facility in Tennessee for two years. The company fired and rehired Ben several times during my seven years as an employee.

Will Cheatham was the next manager/trainer foisted on me and my buyers. Will, an unpleasant man who praised himself with nearly every sentence he spoke, was intense and assertive. Will's verbal habit of ending each sentence with "and everything" annoyed me and everyone around him. He came with his own sales agenda: Promote. Promote. Promote.

"Do *not* waste time with products," he counseled me. "These Archie Bunkers don't care how a product works—they only want a gift and everything."

He was wrong about customers, and I didn't take him to any of my established accounts. We made new calls together where he offered cheap jewelry from China as a promotion and slickly sold eight cases of penetrating lube or hand cleaner to small accounts that needed just one case of twelve.

My protests were ignored, so later I called the swindled buyers and offered to pick up excess products. Yes, I lost my commission and was responsible for freight charges, but I knew these customers would purchase from me for years. I pleaded with upper management to keep their manglers, but they insisted I could learn better sales techniques from their professionals.

Al K. Holic was my next tormentor. Even though obese, he fancied himself a muscleman who worked out daily. Al was addicted to Waffle House coffee with three sugars and could seldom be spotted without a cup of brew in his hand.

"I would rather keep our calls in areas where a Waffle House is located because it's the only coffee I drink." Al's coffee habit ruined my plans for him to visit a variety of customers and return home with a profitable sales day. We spent the bulk of our time stopping for a cup of joe and then waiting for Al to eliminate the liquid. This, plus his insistence on hour-and-a-half lunches and Happy Hour before five p.m., didn't leave much time for sales.

I did, however, learn new products and different types of accounts from Al. His favorite call was to school lunchroom managers. After I learned these women could purchase, I enjoyed over fifty school cafeteria customers. Yes, Al taught me what to demonstrate to these women, but what he failed to mention to them distressed me. As he offered managers trinkets, he wrote several "future ship" orders, shipping the same products to each account for the next two months.

Many cases were returned to Atlanta, and invoices were voided. I assured my lunchroom managers, "This mistake was a shipping error and will not happen again, and no, I will never bring that manager back." They remained loyal to me.

The company soon fired Al for sexually harassing saleswomen he trained, and in my fourth year with the company, Phil Meaup became the National Sales Manager. Phil called me from the airport one Sunday night at eleven o'clock to inform me he was in town and would work with me the next morning. Unhappily, I picked him up at the airport for a day of cold-calling, only to learn that he was in Knoxville to ask me to become a district sales manager.

> *To My Customers,*
>
> *Due to my independent positions as a sales manager and sales rep, I have decided to limit my time for my convenience.*
>
> *At the present, it pleases me to call on you Tuesday and Thursday between 2 pm and 4 pm, probably by phone. This will allow me to start and extend my weekends without interruptions. It will permit me to devote my mornings to recreation such as golf.*
>
> *NOTE: The above regulations apply only as long as business is good. After that, I will be around kissing your ass as usual.*
>
> *Thanks,*
>
> *Your Regional Sales Mangler*

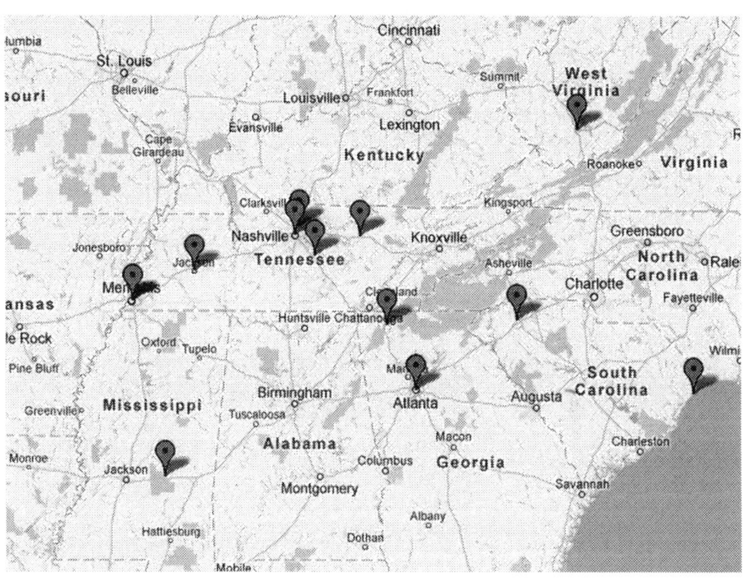

Territory - Womanager

Chapter 7
Womanager

Women aren't as mere as they used to be.

—Walt Kelly, American cartoonist

Although I was flattered by Phil's offer to be the company's first woman manager, I vacillated for a couple of weeks before deciding that the promotion to district manager might provide an opportunity to teach my philosophy of sales to virgin chemical reps. Also, the position offered a damn good compensation package. Vowing not to become a mangler, I accepted the offer despite misgivings about my ability to boss others.

My trainer, Phil, requested I spend one week a month training either new hires in the territory that would be assigned to them or our own salespeople at various stages in their careers. My sales force of eight would soon become thirteen, all of whom I must phone twice a week to monitor their successes and failures. This routine became emotionally and physically draining, especially since I had to maintain my own sales quota.

This pressure intensified after our company president cunningly conceived another time-devouring project. Mr. Mann seemingly believed we managers didn't have enough to do, so he decreed that we should create a monthly newsletter for our salespeople. The content of our paper would include selling tips, our own sales bragging rights, and bravos to anyone who reported a large sale. Harry asked that we take photos of customers advertising our favorite products.

He wanted the six district managers to type, copy, and personally mail newsletters to our teams. (No fax or email available in those years.) Never mind that he sent a company bulletin himself. He didn't seem to do much except sit in his luxurious office micro-managing employees. Our response to his mandate that we also name our paper triggered a reprimand. My colleague in Florida called his newsletter *The Sunshiners*.

"Good name," Harry bragged to my colleague. I lived in East Tennessee, so *Moonshiners* sounded like the perfect title for my articles. Mr. Mann ranted about his distaste for my choice of names, but he finally relented. Two publications later, though, he decided that the newsletters would cease. We moonshiners can handle disappointment.

District managers had no input in hiring, but national sales managers cautioned us not to criticize the hire, lest the recruiter receive disapproval from his superiors. Upper sales management received a substantial bonus for recruitment if the rep lasted a month, so any hire was a good hire for them. My bosses therefore found countless bizarre individuals for me to adopt.

On the positive side, I found the prospect of air travel, swanky hotels, and expense accounts exciting as I awaited news of my first training mission. Atlanta? Miami? New York? No, but I *was* assigned to the tourist mecca of Beckley, West Virginia, to work with a recently hired chemical sales rep. I arrived in Beckley during a February snow mixed with freezing rain and endured a harrowing airplane landing that dodged four-thousand-foot mountains in West Virginia. I didn't want to be there. I wanted to go home.

An attractive young man, Stanley, met me at the airport gate, accompanied by his mother and younger brother. This person was not what I expected—he lived at home and had no previous sales experience. He didn't sound eager or at all ambitious. Only nervous. Like me.

Stanley had completed his assignment of three orders in five days to qualify for one week's training. I reviewed his sales sheet and noted the orders had been from funeral homes only. I insisted we diversify his prospects, later reluctantly agreeing to visit a mortuary. Because I'd never called on a funeral business, I let Stanley take the call in an attempt to make a sale. In his pitch to the mortuary director, Stanley questioned him about the crematorium, which was in the same building.

Stanley boasted, "We sell an excellent oven cleaner."

I never called on another funeral home. Stan worked for another month, and I never heard from him again. Guess he ran out of funeral homes

My company's new harasser sent a trainee, Jade, who sported strumpet stilettos, a tiny, shiny skirt, and a face caulked with makeup. After collecting her at the airport, I deposited her at a motel and asked her to be ready to work (I used the term loosely) at seven a.m. the next day. Jade didn't appear in the lobby the next morning; she didn't answer her room phone. I banged on the door for a minute, and finally her alcohol breath beat her to the entrance.

Wearing a see-through negligee, she squinted at me and complained, "Sugar, I have a terrible hangover. Can we work tomorrow instead?" The man in her bed waved hello, and Jade closed the door.

I changed her plane ticket and sent her home. Soon after, I learned the manager who hired Jade had met her in a bar. He gave her the fictional three orders required to keep the job, along with two weeks' draw. I could only guess his motive.

My next assignment was in Memphis, a short flight from home. I flew to Memphis one wintry day to train Janice, "an experienced salesperson," assured my manager. She met me at the airport, her jacket held together by enormous safety pins. Janice wore pink hair clips in blue-tinted tresses. It was her task to plan our workweek as I had never been to the area.

Janice's proposal included two days at Graceland, one day at the Peabody Hotel watching the duck march, and each night partying on Beale Street. Janice pleaded, "My husband, Rodney, wants to come along with us to Graceland. He would also like to work with us to see how you sell chemicals."

"My job is to train you in chemical sales, not to be entertained," I insisted.

"But we could have so much fun in Memphis, and I've never been to

Graceland."

"No and no."

The two of us—no husband in tow—worked a grueling week throughout West Memphis, Arkansas, and northern Mississippi. We opened several accounts while Janice whined in the background about her need to see Elvis's bedroom. During the week, I learned that her only sales experience had been selling burial plots. She wrote orders for a few chemicals, but not enough to cover her draw. She resigned a month later. Management was not at all what I'd expected it to be.

Teaching new hires about our chemical products was essential if they planned on a career with my company. Educating them about which people could order products and where to find their places of business could be a demanding process. If you add to those tasks the teaching of sales techniques, training a novice salesperson presented a substantial challenge.

I lost many sales when a rookie salesperson rode with me to call on new accounts. A proven closing technique involved asking the customer a key closing question from a pool of several possibilities:

"How many cases can you use today?"

"Would you rather have a 20-gallon pail or a 35-gallon drum?"

"What is your shipping address?"

The idea was to ask the question and then SHUT UP! If the customer spoke first, then he had bought the product, but if the salesperson said anything, the sale was lost. My trainees and I practiced this technique many times before going into an account, but more than a few couldn't tolerate the silence after I asked the closing question.

I inquired of the buyer, "Would you rather purchase your grease in tubes or buckets?" There might be a few seconds of silence before my trainee would invariably ask something like, "Are those photos on your desk your kids? They sure are cute." And the sale flew out the window.

Many times, I gently kicked my new salesperson as she questioned our customer, but usually it was too late.

The manager's practice of hiring anyone who could fog a mirror and hoping one out of ten would be successful was rarely effective, wasting company time and money. In fairness, it was difficult for anyone to predict who would be ambitious enough to become a well-paid salesperson. This was a tough, competitive industry.

Even with my laughable experiences in training, fortunately I worked with several individuals who were eager to become successful in chemical sales. Several of those people became good friends. One woman earned enough commission to open her own art studio.

Friends and family alike often asked, "If you're a manager, can I work for you? It looks easy." Folks who tried sales only to realize customers don't automatically come with the job lasted but a few weeks and sometimes only a day.

My sister, Nancy, worked with me two days until we encountered a rude customer who practically shouted, "Where the hell is my coil cleaner? Maintenance is out of it!" I nicely explained that I stocked a few cases in my garage and promised to return within the hour with his order. Nancy suggested that buyers should order what they might need in plenty of time. Sales was not for her.

My good friend, Eleanor, worked with me only one day; an ill-mannered purchasing agent asked us to get out of her office before I could even offer her a business card. Eleanor now contentedly works with computers in an office. Kelly, my then twenty-two-year-old daughter, found herself between jobs and decided if I could sell chemicals, so could she. I encouraged her, hoping she could eventually build a profitable career for herself.

We drove to Crossville, TN, across Cumberland Mountain, marveling at lush scenery. Our first call at a church went well when the custodian purchased a large quantity of floor products.

Cumberland County Highway Department, a new call, sent us to the garage to meet their newly hired maintenance supervisor. Willy, chewing a mouthful of tobacco, sat in a greasy, junk-filled office—typical of vehicle garages. The rubbery smell of newly purchased tires permeated the building. Kelly coughed, choked, held her nose, and headed for my car. It was her first and last day in sales.

I offered my younger daughter, Cheryl, part of my territory if she would try chemical sales. Already an experienced salesperson, Cheryl opened several accounts. Customers purchased more products from her than they ever

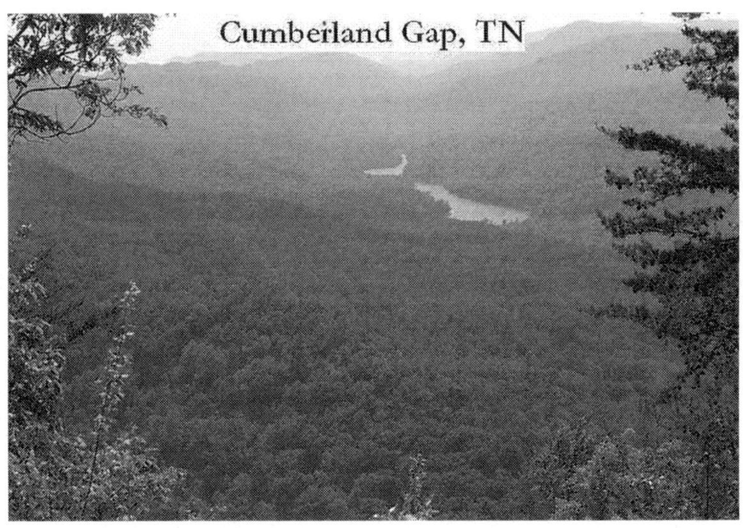
Cumberland Gap, TN

had from me. She was personable, knowledgeable, and genuinely likeable. My daughter left chemical sales when I resigned from the company in Atlanta and joined me later when I started my own company. Coincidentally, she applied for and received a job at the same grocery supply company I left years earlier. She enjoyed a successful career in food service.

Kelly's boyfriend at the time, Kenny Siao, waited tables while saving to open his own restaurant. Kenny, a native of Malaysia, imagined a decent commission from sales would supplement his waiter's tips. His large circle of friends and family, many of them owners and managers of Asian restaurants, surely would keep him supplied in customers. Kenny didn't realize that restaurants rarely purchase expensive chemicals, as they are operating to make profits. Most eateries use one supplier for their dish machine soap—whatever company can maintain the equipment.

I went with Kenny for a few weeks, calling on new accounts. His personality and looks made up for his lack of experience, and most buyers welcomed him, even if they didn't buy much of anything. Kenny hated cold-calling. He came to visit me one night and confessed, "I go to a movie every day so I won't have to make these calls. I can't do this anymore."

Kenny saved his money and opened Stir Fry Café in Knoxville and several other successful restaurants. He succeeded in procuring two of my biggest accounts, which I kept until I retired.

I was conflicted about management. I enjoyed most of the training and opening new accounts, but I lacked the ability to discipline my sales people by withholding draw or criticizing them.

Harry Mann, our company president, stood small in stature but barked when he spoke. He presented himself as myopic and brusque. His balding head sported a toupee resembling a ferret, and he usually wore a shiny, green suit to meetings. Harry offered suggestions for improving my management skills.

"Diana, I don't believe you're tough enough with these people. Your biggest problem is your soft voice. It doesn't command respect. Work on developing a deeper voice."

"The better to speak to you, My Dear," said The Big Bad Wolf.

Mr. Mann insisted that female managers and sales reps wear dresses or skirts when working in the field. I explained that we called on dirty garages. Sometimes we walked through construction sites or climbed to a rooftop to check a cooling tower. Pants were more practical and less revealing. He advised us to carry jeans in our sample cases and change in the customer's restroom. I assumed he had never been in a garage mechanics' toilet area.

I called each person in my group twice a week and more often if anyone wasn't meeting the arbitrary quota set by the company president. The established method was to berate and belittle our sales teams to make them sell more while questioning each call they made that didn't result in an order. Sales meetings were held monthly for district and regional managers, where we in turn were criticized for not pushing our reps far enough. The meetings were torturous, but I earned more than $75,000 a year, including commissions, in the mid '80s, so I followed the rules—most of the time.

As I drove up to the company building for my first district manager's meeting, I immediately noted the amusing parking area adornments. As Monty Hall had explained in his hiring interview, the company was one of Cadillacs and swimming pools. I never saw the swimming pools, although each prime parking spot for president, vice presidents, and regional managers boasted a Cadillac, each new El Dorado more ostentatious than the next. Gold hood ornaments, gold trim, and gold grills made the exterior of the office look like a pimp convention.

District sales management eventually included two more women. We three were also the top sellers of all the sixteen-person management groups and numbers two, three, and four in the entire sixty-person sales force. At one particular district meeting, a salesman who never reached his quota said, "I would like to know how much money the women made this year."

Obviously, we each made considerably more than any salesman at the meeting, including sales commissions and extra compensation as managers. The next week, the females were fired from management. We were told that the supervisors believed our jobs were too demanding, but privately a few of the men told us of complaints to the national sales manager. "It's not fair for women to bring in more money than men." Soon after, the company assigned me my own mangler, who addressed me as "Gal."

Vicki, Lisa, and I—the three, fired sales managers—were angry. We discussed filing a discrimination lawsuit, but this era was before Anita Hill, and unfair treatment of minority groups didn't seem unusual. The other women managers thought they would cause trouble, a typical response from women in business who had lived through the '60's.

My company treated all employees to a dinner once a year, where our company president bestowed awards and trophies for top salespeople. In previous years, I received a number of accolades both for sales and management, based on a capricious quota that no one fully understood.

The last banquet I attended in 1986 found me out of favor with Mr. Mann. A friend and I spent a week in Cancun, Mexico, that year. One week turned into about sixteen days when Hurricane Gilbert visited Mexico and delayed all flights out of the country. Not only did I fail to make quota by losing over two week's sales, but I also had been relieved of management duties.

Management found a new way to humiliate folks who failed to make the required number of sales: chicken! Yes, those esteemed sales reps received steak and champagne for dinner and sat at the head table with company officers. Unworthy folks were served chicken and iced tea at a small table by the door. I further angered Harry when I paid the server $20 to bring my husband a steak because he didn't like chicken.

The final assault on my dignity began when our national sales manager interviewed one of my competitors, Mary Ann. She sold chemicals in most of my accounts, so we strove for the same sales. Phil Meaup explained his devious idea in attempting to hire her. She and I would share accounts, and whoever beat the other one to the customer with any product kept that sale.

I protested, "These are my customers, and I shouldn't have to share them. The customers surely won't want to keep up with which products they purchased from me and which they bought from Lisa. We'll look foolish vying to outsell each other at our customers' expense." No matter, the deal was done. Except that Mary Ann also thought the idea a ridiculous one and refused the offer.

Because of the humiliating dismissal from management, along with several months of "computer problems" resulting in my not receiving full commission checks and sometimes no check at all, I resigned from my position. I had been with this company for seven years.

The Georgia-based company continues to be successful. Many of their salespeople stay for years, enjoying enviable commissions. As a result of my experiences in management, I recognized the bizarre treatment of our sales force and knew I'd been unjustly removed from my managerial role.

An Indiana chemical company contacted me and six other reps from my company who also weren't receiving full commission checks. Our contracts stated we couldn't sell any product to any customer within our existing territories for a period of two years after leaving, so our new company paid an undisclosed fee to purchase our contracts. We were hired. My new company provided a pleasant place to work, and the bosses were hands-off. After five good years, I learned they planned to sell the company to the largest chemical supplier in the country. I resigned because that firm already had several successful reps in my area.

"What now?"

Some of my co-workers had opened their own companies and offered to help me if I wanted to do the same. Tired of job interviews, managers, and manglers, the idea of being my own boss tempted me. Every customer I'd developed over the years had changed over to the company in Indiana with me. Would they accept me again if I started my own business?

It was time to find a new adventure.

North Carolina Mountains

Chapter 8
I Was Once Owned By a Small Business

Always do whatever's next.

—George Carlin

My new journey into business ownership could easily have become a misadventure. I knew nothing about operating a small business. I neither understood accounting nor had any computer skills. Panic and pressure threatened to barge in and take over, but somehow my office began to function. Many days I considered quitting and wanted to weep, but I'd spent my quota of tears years ago, so the business marched onward.

My former co-workers flooded me with price lists and catalogs from various chemical suppliers, and I was astonished at the minimal costs of products I'd been selling. A case of twelve aerosols cost about $18 and sold for over $100. A $25 gallon of chemical carried a wholesale price of $6 or less. With none of my commission paying for company Cadillacs and deluxe office buildings, I would soon be affluent if only I could maintain control of this venture.

Master Card, Visa, and I were ready to begin, though I was not prepared for countless expenses: office furniture and supplies, county and state licenses, company pamphlets, and a second telephone line dedicated to the business. I purchased batches of promotional items displaying our company logo.

My garage had sufficient storage until I decided to private label products. Private labeling meant designing my own label to insure competitors could not sell the same generic item to my customers, which forced me to order eighteen to thirty-six cases of product at one time. Added expenses included renting storage from a local business and paying to have a shed built next to our garage, which served as a pick-up and drop-off point for UPS.

One advantage of labeling products was that I named them. Citrus degreaser became Big Orange, and I called orange deodorizer Orange Lady. During the University of Tennessee's football and basketball seasons, orange products sold well because of the orange and white school colors. UT had earned the nickname Big Orange. I thought about naming an insecticide "Say No to Bugs," but Nancy Reagan's popularity had come and gone.

During my first year of business ownership, I wrote invoices and purchase orders with paper and pen. Computers began appearing on my customers' desks, so I knew my business would function smoother with newer technology. I rented an overpriced desktop system that I slowly and painfully learned to use, and I purchased accounting software.

Hours of paperwork cost me time on the road selling products, so my friend of thirty years, Mary, came to work part time. She phoned customers and suppliers. She shipped and received products. Mary became an invaluable assistant; it would have been difficult to manage my business without her. She joined me on customer calls to familiarize herself with my accounts.

Often, buyers and other employees would ask, "When is Mary coming to visit?" At times, if I answered our office phone, suppliers, customers' secretaries, or purchasing agents who didn't know me would complain.

"I'd rather talk to that purchasing agent / sales manager / credit officer / shipping clerk, Mary. She knows what I need."

Mary and I had been friends in high school, and I had occasionally corrected her homework. I knew she couldn't spell correctly. After I noticed an invoice to Sweetwater Hospital in the outgoing mail, I took charge of typing all invoices. She had spelled the customer's name as "Sweetworter Nusing Home" and addressed it to the "frount" office (front office.) Despite her spelling disability, Mary remained a priceless assistant who made my business life much easier.

Trade associations were another necessary expense. It seemed as if each industry formed its own association. Vendors could join the organizations and either pay dues or rent a booth at an annual trade show to display their products. The County Highway Officials Association, the Tennessee Association of School Superintendents, and the Government Housing Authorities Directors Association constituted only a few organizations with prospective customers who asked me if my company would like to purchase a booth at their annual trade show. School bus garage superintendents and school cafeteria supervisors promoted yearly seminars and invited vendors to attend with samples.

Mary and I attended at least one trade fair a year, often in Gatlinburg. These events usually spanned three days, and, to spare the expense of a hotel, we drove home each night and returned the next morning. I paid about $200 for each booth and ordered expensive company logo favors. We purchased a banner, and then spent all day pushing our products. I acquired several new customers from our efforts.

We hoped vendors wouldn't realize what a small operation we were, so Mary and I became purchasing agents, accounts payable / receivable, office managers, shipping clerks, and often warehouse managers—whatever the situation required. One morning I spoke with the vice president of a large firm, Hal Hanson, while getting ready for work in my bathroom. Not thinking, I turned on my hair dryer. When it buzzed in my buyer's ear, Mr. Hanson demanded, "What's that noise?"

"I'm in our warehouse," I offered. "A forklift just went by."

Piles of profits didn't pour in at first, but advantages outweighed expenses. I floundered happily on my own, and I could sell just about anything my customers needed. Safety equipment, paper products, turf equipment, grease guns, and gloves became part of my line.

Manglers with their requirements of detailed daily customer reports, phone calls, and general harassment were never missed. I never yearned for

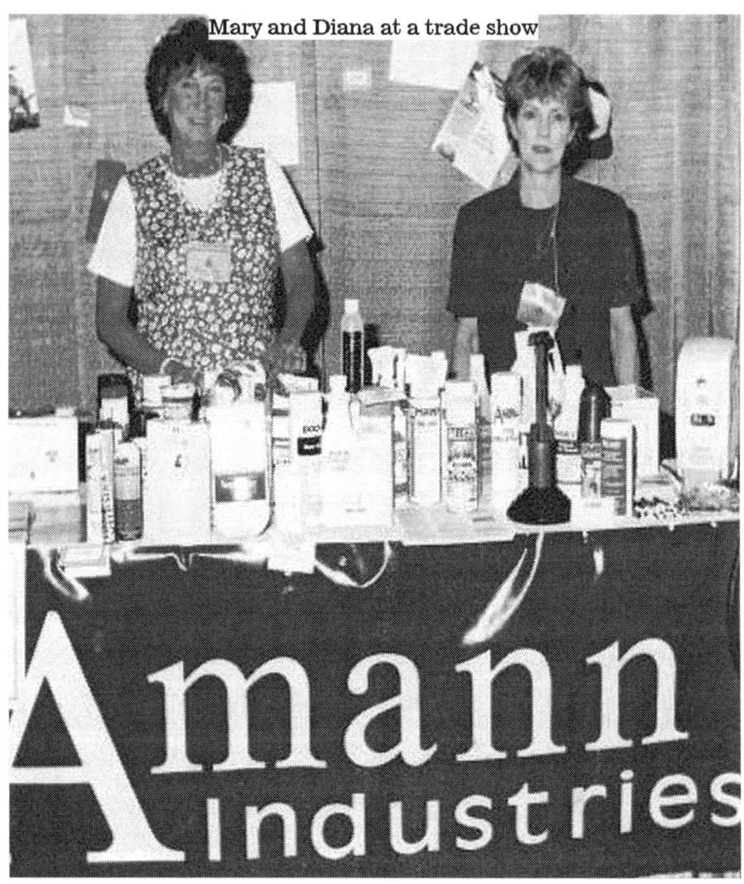

Mary and Diana at a trade show

the trophies I'd won for sales and management. They found their way to a flea market, but I longingly dreamed of vacations earned during my tenures with various employers.

I once won a vacation to New Orleans as a prize from the tobacco company. A food distributor awarded me a trip to Cincinnati to watch the Reds and Braves at Riverfront Stadium. When employed by the two chemical companies, I won paid vacations to Las Vegas, New Orleans, Aruba, Acapulco, and twice to Cancun, St. Thomas, Hawaii, and Jamaica. Would my small business afford me the same travel opportunities? It would if I could find time to leave my business. Days flashed by, hectic and overflowing with work.

Allow me to describe a typical day in my life as a small business owner:

> *Early in the morning, I call suppliers to order chemicals, and then begin driving to Jamestown or maybe Jonesboro, Tennessee, to make sales calls. Thirty miles on the way to my first customer, I find a phone booth to check messages. I finally own a cell phone, but service fails to reach all areas. A trucking company has left a message to tell me thirty-six cases of penetrating oil that is not supposed to be here until next week is on its way to my place of business.*
>
> *Truckers' unions have ruled that drivers are not required to unload shipments. If Mary isn't in the office today, I must backtrack to meet the driver at our storage unit and unload his truck while he watches and chain-smokes. I stop at my garage to drop off today's deliveries and samples from my car so I can fit a dolly in the car that I'll need to unload the shipment.*
>
> *Eight cases of just delivered cargo have been ordered by a school maintenance supervisor in Sevierville, so I repack my car and deliver to him, because he pays within a week and my cash flow is tight. As I leave Sevier County, I spot the only phone booth that usually works, but a vandal has cut the receiver from the cord. Sevierville courthouse has a working pay phone, and I stand while prisoners awaiting trial finish their calls.*
>
> *The next message is from a customer in Crossville, Tennessee.*
>
> *"Help, I'm out of ice-melting compound. A blizzard's been predicted for our area. Please bring me three hundred pounds ASAP." Customers never order products they need for winter until snow is on its way, and then they panic and expect immediate delivery.*
>
> *Since my car isn't large enough to carry 50-pound drums of calcium chloride (ice melt), I rush home to borrow my husband's van, head to the storage unit, and offer the clerk $50 if she'll help me load six drums of product. We struggle to load the containers in Wayne's van. I drive,*

terrified and sliding over Cumberland Mountain in a snowstorm, to Crossville, Tennessee, to save their sidewalks from an icy demise.

As I leave Cumberland County and again check messages, a client complains that he hasn't received his wastewater degreaser and needs it at once. I locate the barrel, still at AAA trucking, but the dispatcher saysit cannot be delivered until next week. I call Mary. She and her husband, Harland, drive to the trucking company, load a 35-gallon drum of degreaser in their truck, and deliver it to my customer's wastewater treatment plant.

The buyer complains, "This is not what I ordered." The chemical matches his purchase order. "You need to take this drum back and bring me the right thing." After several phone calls and faxing a copy of his purchase order, he grudgingly agrees to keep the drum. His company doesn't pay the invoice for three months. The next time I see him he brags, "Your competitor gave me a shotgun for Christmas."

The next day, the University of Tennessee calls with a complaint. Their purchasing agent had ordered a 35-gallon drum of liquid ice-melting compound, but the agent received thirty-five 1-gallon jugs instead. Mary issues a pick-up and reorders the correct product. Meanwhile, I have a flat tire in Newport, Tennessee. My spare tire is underneath a heavy product load. I must unpack my products and drop them in the street in order to retrieve my spare. A policeman stops and tells me I'm blocking traffic. He waits with folded arms while I change the tire and reload my chemicals.

Each day proved unique. I thrived on chaos. The more bizarre this job became, the more I seemed to sell. My buyers remained happy to receive personal deliveries without freight charges, and they were proud of my business ownership. Elusive serendipity came by and lingered awhile: if I made sales calls all day and sold nothing, I would inevitably receive a substantial order by phone or a faxed purchase order back at my home office. This phenomenon would continue for fifteen years, and even though I had developed a comfortable customer base, new accounts were essential to keep my company profitable. After five years on my own, I won a bid and acquired thirteen new customers in Campbell County, Tennessee, situated between Cumberland Plateau in the northeast and the Appalachian Ridge and Valley Range in the southeast

This is how I won the bid, competing with "Big Boys" of the chemical industry:

School cafeterias provided a large chunk of my clients who enjoyed buying privileges without obtaining purchase orders. Lunchroom managers knew their schoolchildren's tastes and understood employees' cleaning-product needs. Cooks ordered food and other supplies accordingly.

Sometime in the '90s, government felt it necessary to bid all items schools purchased, wrongly thinking those in charge couldn't buy correctly. As a result, I lost all my lunchroom accounts. I stopped to visit a friend, the school lunch program supervisor in Campbell County, and she told me one of my competitors won the bid for chemical supplies. I was surprised since the competing company carried extremely expensive products.

"We chose your competitor, even though his bid was higher than our food supplier, because his products are safe," my friend told me. "We've paid several workers' compensation suits in the past year because of injuries from hazardous chemicals."

The fact that the other company delivered harmless products did not ring true, so I investigated by requesting a look at Material Safety Data Sheets, or MSDS, from each product purchased. This request lay within my rights as a potential bidder. Each school lunchroom was required to keep a book with a copy of MSDS for every product stocked in each facility. Upon viewing all MSDS in each school, I discovered no data at all listing chemical ingredients, hazards, or safety warnings as required by OSHA (Occupational Health and Safety Administration). The safety books contained only papers advertising the winning bidders' products with information on how well they worked—no safety information, no hazardous warnings.

I also learned of some dangerous products that had been bid as safe to use, including caustic oven cleaner touted as benign and chlorine bleach listed as harmless. Aerosol stainless-steel cleaner had been recorded as "liquid" when the bid asked for no aerosols.

I found many more discrepancies, but a master MSDS book located in central office apparently had never been read. After I listed these major problems, researched chemical compounds, and presented my findings to food supervisors and school finance directors, they cancelled the previous bid, rebid with new instructions, and Amann Industries received the contract to supply thirteen school cafeterias.

My motivation certainly included obtaining school business, but more than that, I was angry that my customers had been duped and were using products that could harm them.

Our bid included providing these lunchrooms with warewashing products, drain enzymes, disinfectants, and general cleaners. There was one onerous caveat: this bid requested *dispensers* for dish machines, hand soap, toilet paper, and drain enzymes. And so my list grew and grew. The task of acquiring not only equipment but products as well seemed overwhelming.

County finance departments chose the lowest bidder this time; therefore, I couldn't afford to hire a mechanic to install dispensers. Don, my son-in-law, and, Harland, Mary's husband worked for a small fee. A local supplier agreed to manufacturer certain chemicals to my specs, although the availability of numerous products already existed with various suppliers.

But what to do about the requirement of weekly delivery to each individual school that ordered product? I understood, unhappily, that my small Honda CRV would become a delivery vehicle, along with help from Mary. We received faxed orders Friday for Monday deliveries. We then printed invoices, loaded my car, reordered products as needed, and delivered to thirteen schools.

The cases and pails I carried into each cafeteria weighed between eighteen and forty-five pounds. When my loaded car, packed nearly to the ceiling, left no room for Mary, I delivered alone. Three years after I begin delivering to school lunchrooms, my husband, Wayne, bought a red (neck) pickup truck and helped me load and deliver.

I learned to install dispensers and repair the smaller equipment. We located an electrician in Campbell County who maintained warewashing instruments. "Lunchroom ladies" became friends, and I enjoyed a good relationship with most of them.

Amann Industries Rules:

1. The customer is always right.

2. If the customer is wrong, see Rule Number 1.

School kitchen loading dock

Chapter 9
Customers: The Good, the Bad and the Frugal

There is hardly anything in the world that some man cannot make a little worse and sell a little cheaper, and the people who consider price only are this man's lawful prey.

—John Ruskin, English author and critic

Taking care of the school bid became a full-time job, though I managed to visit my other customers. Crises from school kitchens arose nonstop, and repairs or adjustments were a daily chore.

I bought a drill, battery tester, and toolbox. Plumbing tape filled my pockets. Local hardware stores supplied me with plastic tubing for drain dispensers and 6-volt batteries that I had to rewire because those without a spring-top to fit the equipment were difficult to locate.

Frequently, I climbed under sinks to repair drain tubing dispensers—they dripped an enzyme to prevent kitchen grease from solidifying, thus resulting in a floor drain overflow—or on top of an industrial dish machine to reset its timer.

Stooping under a pot-and-pan sink in a high-school kitchen, I moved old utensils and metal shelves out of the way so I could refill a pail of drain

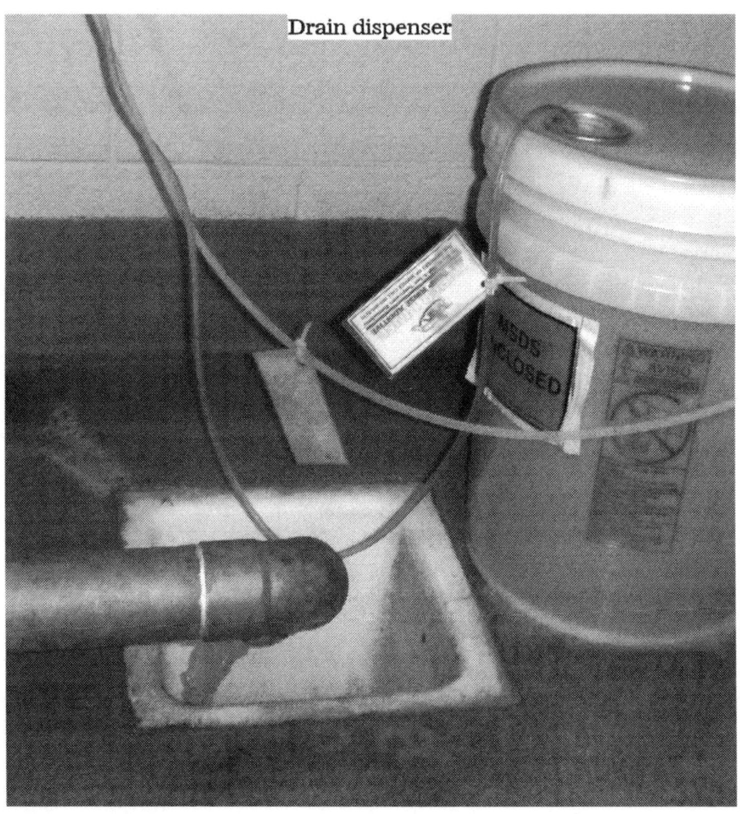

Drain dispenser

enzyme. Alice, a seventy-year-old cook, whispered, "They's a jar of home brew hid back of them metal shelves. It's mine, so please don't go tellin' the manager." I kept her secret.

Managers called or paged me frequently. Although many malfunctions occurred because the kitchen equipment had become old and needed costly repair, a few employees created their own difficulties.

When the women used too much soap and didn't rinse trays prior to inserting them in the machine, this triggered more chemical input. The pot-and-pan soap used in the hand sink irritated their hands. I provided rubber gloves at no charge, but no one liked to wear them. They insisted the smell of our odor-free mopping solution made them ill.

I provided samples until we found a cleaner the managers liked, but some cooks still insisted their throats were "closing" from the smell. As if on cue, several women would grab their throats to demonstrate choking. Meanwhile, the burning odor of chlorine they poured into mopping solutions caused *my* throat to close.

Lunchroom ladies continued to be some of my best customers. The southern Appalachian region offered a variety of other prospects. I vowed to unearth them all. Municipal electrical departments, fire, police, and especially water and wastewater departments employed mostly friendly people.

Silt Happens, a poster in one wastewater treatment plant, greeted me as I entered the building. I soon learned these customers would be friendly. Often bored, they welcomed company from elsewhere. Plant operators enjoyed generous purchase order limits and could use most of my chemical products. Every town had at least one treatment plant, and I found friends in many of them.

Walking into a timeworn elementary school, nostalgia flooded my senses. Hardwood floors, buffed and burnished, still exposed their age. Visions of little girls in Mary Jane shoes, boys wearing starched pants, and schoolteachers whose dresses hung below the knees greeted me as I entered. Odors of chalkboards and erasers sent my mind spinning to my old school, now replaced by modern office buildings.

An abundance of public and private schools populated the counties in my territory. They turned into a loyal customer base, but public education systems had little extra money. School customers used money from children's photo sales, soft drink machines, and Christmas promotions to purchase extra supplies.

Do you want to speak with the principal or the secretary who is the only person who know what's going on? This poster in an elementary school office greeted me. Talking my way into the principal's office invited rejection. Faculty secretaries protected their principal from unwanted visitors. The first few times I called on a principal, I felt as if I had been caught cutting class and now sat waiting for a reprimand. But whenever a principal invited me to speak with the school custodian, I anticipated a nice order.

School custodians knew that products sent to them from a countywide bid often were ineffective and even harmful to employees and their facility. I have seen employees with burns on their hands caused by cheap acid cleaner. Many times, shoddy floor-care chemicals ruined floors. Stainless steel flush valves and bathroom faucets peeled because the custodian used an acid toilet-bowl cleaner on them.

A faucet cleaned with non-acid cleaner

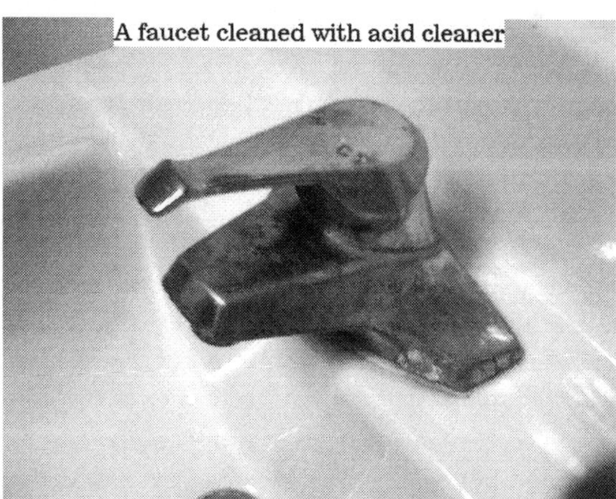
A faucet cleaned with acid cleaner

Coy, an elementary school head custodian, won the principal's approval by keeping the school immaculate. He was allowed to order what he needed. A large man with a square face and white hair, his sense of humor kept the teachers, principals, and children laughing. Coy became my friend and loyal customer for twenty-five years. I now visit him in his retirement home. "What did you bring me?" he asks when I arrive. I always take a small gift, like a hat or pocket knife, as I did when he worked as custodian.

Coy, like many of my Appalachian customers, acted as a part-time pastor, and he would often summarize a recent sermon for me. I enjoyed listening to him. His passionate, colorful speech motivated those who heard his words.

Country gospel singers were also plentiful in my territory. A few singers even brought their cassette tapes to work so I could buy them. *Lois and the Virginians* riveted listeners with twangy tales of treachery and sorrowful songs of sinfulness.

As I traveled in rural areas, I learned about these folks who can trace their religious roots to revival preaching and folk ways of the mountains. Mountain traditions, music, stories, and lifestyles were important factors in shaping the religious experience of the region, according to *Foxfire 7* (Inc. Foxfire Fund 1982). Diversity remained abundant in the customers I found and in the businesses where they worked.

Hospitals, nursing homes, and assisted-living facilities became a source of multiple sales. "We are the downstairs people who hold up the rest of the building," Judy, the head housekeeper at a small town hospital, told me. Often, underpaid personnel were located in lower levels. Maintenance employees, housekeepers, laundry employees, and kitchen staff insured that the facility functioned. Upper floors with administrators, accounting, and purchasing agents seldom saw the work that made their jobs possible.

Government housing became a source of income for me as well as a shocking revelation. My first housing customer, Jake, who was head of maintenance, asked me to accompany him as he sought a product to clean the bathtub in one recently vacated housing unit. A small but muscular man and an excellent electrician, he ended each sentence with, "Dontcha know?"

"This unit we're goin' in is a shit hole, dontcha know?" I did know. I saw walls covered in roaches and a tub so black it might have been spray painted.

It was simply filthy. My suggestion would have been to burn the place, but the property belonged to the government. I needed to find a cleaner that would suffice. I demonstrated a product to clean his tubs, and Jake ordered several chemicals from me. After each of my visits to these housing units, I drove straight home and took a shower.

The first unit Jake had shown me was not government housing's only problem. One particular apartment appeared ghastly. The family who lived there had been evicted after loud fighting, so I expected a mess. My expectations proved correct. Most low-income housing I visited contained carpeting that maintenance personnel cleaned or replaced after tenants moved. The fighting couple, obviously heavy smokers, used the carpet as an ashtray. Not only did cigarette ashes cover the rugs, but the renters had actually put their cigarettes out by squashing them into the carpet.

I observed messes rivaling the unique ashtray several times during my years of sales. These examples were exceptions; most housing residents I met kept their units clean and were grateful for help.

Purchasing agents could make life difficult for an honest sales rep and even harder for employees who needed my products. The attitude seemed to be, "I don't care if it is concentrated, or delivered on time with thirty days payable. I want the *cheapest.*" Buyers who weren't end users couldn't assume that less costly products would function as promised.

A solid waste facility became one of my solid customers, purchasing lubricants, gear oil, hand cleaners, and deodorizers for their garbage trucks until the county hired a purchasing agent to save county money. The PA, a retired Army drill sergeant, had his own ideas of cutting costs.

At that time diesel cost much less than gas, so Mister Penny-pincher ordered the solid waste garage's underground tank filled with the wrong fuel. Diesel instead of gas. Months passed before the tanks could safely be cleaned and refilled with gas. In the meantime, county trucks purchased fuel at a local service station, which cost the county several times more than expected savings.

Any facility that serviced vehicles benefited from quality non-melt, high-temp lubricants. Mechanics knew which lubricants prolonged equipment life. However, purchasing agents frequently vetoed the more expensive products.

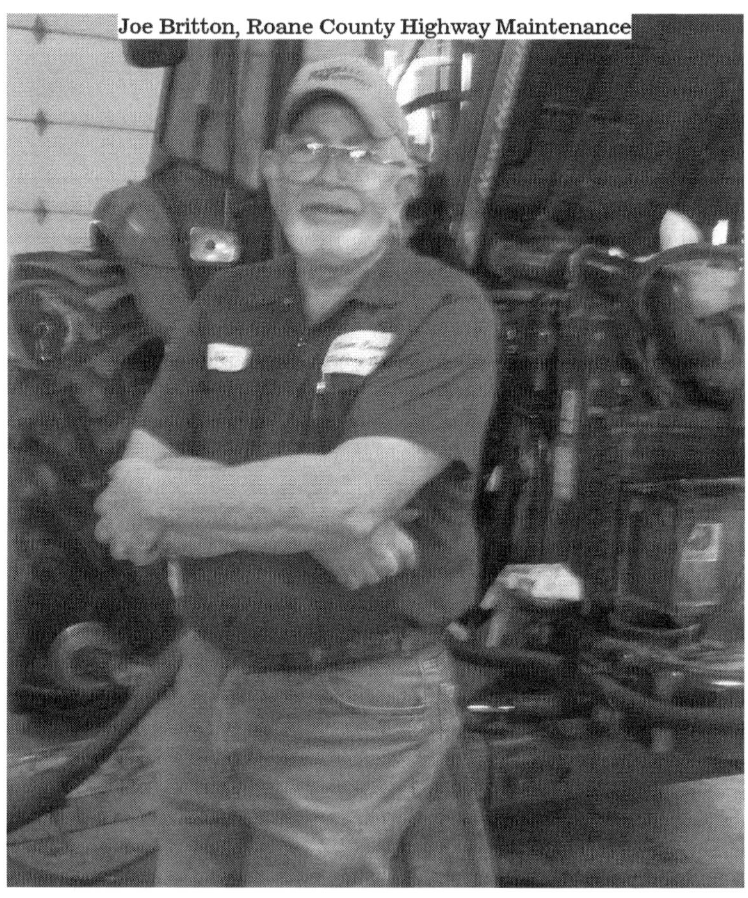
Joe Britton, Roane County Highway Maintenance

Deodorizers listed among my best-selling chemicals and I took delight in each new fragrance my company formulated. Mulberry, Citrus, Cinnamon, Fresh Linen, Honeysuckle, Mango—each new odor more enticing than the last. Oddly, men more often choose Baby Powder or Cherry, while Linen or Fresh Laundry was the favorite of women. Fellow sales reps alike hated Pine—we called it Jail house smell. Employees in any business enjoyed choosing a favorite smell. Prison and jail restrooms stank, so they were all excellent prospects for odor control chemicals.

Brushy Mountain Prison in Petros, Tennessee, a formidable fortress set against Brushy Mountain, built in 1896 and closed in 2009, housed felons serving lengthy or life sentences. The prison consistently purchased smell-good products. Guards and trustees settled on a cherry fragrance since it performed well in covering malodors.

When I opened my company, I purchased the chemical that I'd previously sold to Brushy from the same supplier, but the maker had discontinued adding pink coloring to the liquid. Loud complaints from end-users told me that the product smelled different. It no longer effectively removed disagreeable odors.

Not wanting to lose the orders, Mary, my part-time help, and I opened each quart bottle of product, added three drops of red food coloring, re-sealed them, and delivered four to eight cases every couple of weeks to Brushy. The product worked much better when pink.

Perry, a prison trustee serving a life sentence for killing a man in a bar fight, was an African-American man in his sixties. He wore wire-rim glasses to match his wiry frame. His hair resembled dandelion puffballs on each side of his head. Perry counted as his friend another inmate, James Earl Ray, who served a life sentence for killing Martin Luther King, Jr. Ray died in Brushy in 1998.

He took me to see the buyer whenever I visited the prison. Perry and I became friends, and I supplied him with cigarette lighters and ball caps. He advised me on products that correctional facilities prohibited. These forbidden products included acid chemicals, like drain opener and oven cleaner. Prisons didn't allow any chemical containing isopropyl alcohol, like window cleaner, for example. Inmates strained it through bread and drank it to get high.

Perry told me the story of one particular prisoner. "Poor man, he tried to drink sulfuric acid drain opener. It burned his throat so severely he lost his voice."

When a competitor threatened to take some of my business, Perry told him the buyer was not available. After the rep started a rumor that buyers purchased my products only because I slept with them, Perry asked me, "Want me and some boys to play *Deliverance* with him?" He surely joked; prisons didn't allow banjos.

Customers became friends I cherished and looked forward to visiting. If buyers were rude, I didn't have to see them again. Harassers weren't common, even if most men hadn't done business with a woman before. With a couple of exceptions, men and women alike treated me with respect, as I did them.

One of the exceptions, a purchaser I met, sat in his office desk chair with his feet not reaching the floor. The diminutive man told me he visited Nashville often. He then posed a question. "How about meeting me in Nashville sometime? We could eat dinner and spend the night in a motel." I never visited him again, but I did take his order for a drum of weed killer.

A facilities director for a small college, an enormous man with a bald head and tiny hands, smugly informed me, "Honey, I never buy from a married woman because you stole the job away from a man." I tactfully explained that four men had worked this territory, but none of them had stayed with our company. I later assigned his account to an unmarried saleswoman who received large orders from him until he propositioned her. She threw an order pad at him and left his office, never to return.

In the same small town as the college, I later found a new customer, the utility department. As I entered the warehouse, a poster greeted me. An image of an old cowboy aiming his rifle warned: *We shoot every third salesman; the first two just left!* "Then I'm safe," I told the buyer, "since I'm a woman." He chuckled and asked me to sit down.

Several employees wandered in, and one of the linemen asked, "Do you have any samples of hand cleaner in your car?"

"Yes, I do. I'll bring in a few different types. As I opened my car door, black grease covered my hand. Leaving the restroom after cleaning up, I found that someone had spread sticky glue on the bathroom doorknob. The employees at the utility department treated each new salesperson to this initiation. These men became friends I'll never forget. They gave me an order each visit, and whenever I visited this facility, I wore pants because they gave me lifts in a bucket truck and let me operate their forklift.

Meetings with customers often felt like social visits. I learned about their families, jobs, and hobbies. Men, and sometimes women, enjoyed discussing fishing and hunting. Because my father had made his living writing about fish and game, I was familiar with these outdoor sports.

Ray, a county school maintenance supervisor, avid hunter, and expert taxidermist, decorated his office with the results of his crafts. Deer and elk heads, squirrels, and snakeskins stared down from every wall. I complimented his newest stuffed game when one creature made me recoil in terror. On Ray's desk lay a lifelike, coiled rattlesnake! His taxidermy skill caused me to shudder. Ray laughed.

"Hell, I pull this trick on all salespeople," he admitted. Ray remained a good customer who purchased from me each time I stopped by. After I retired, I introduced him to Connie, a friend and fellow chemical sales rep. He buys products from her still as I write this book.

Visiting one of my favorite accounts meant a cheery workday. Driving over mountains and through countryside towns never delivered boredom; however, our unpredictable weather could be terribly uncomfortable. Employees at accounts I visited in spring and autumn announced their dismay at working inside while I enjoyed the luxury of traveling through beautiful scenery.

"What's it like outside?" I frequently heard from folks who stayed indoors all day.

Snow, rain, and unbearable heat didn't elicit similar envy. Inclement weather aroused sympathy for me, but bad weather usually didn't keep me homebound. I rarely took a day off from scheduled work.

I grew a bit weary of the same old question whenever outside conditions were miserable. "Did you bring this rain (heat, snow) with you?" Ha-ha, I've heard that question ten times already today.

Secretaries and many purchasing agents who filled me with dread during my first years of chemical sales became friends after I'd visited them a few times. A small novelty or bag of candy produced smiles. A bottle of Maker's Mark brought purchase order numbers. I developed a rapport with the upstairs folks; they supported the supervisors who requested my products.

Several women kept teddy bears I had given them when their children were small. They passed them on to grandchildren, and the women often showed me pictures of their grandkids holding those stuffed animals.

Most of my male buyers amassed quite a knife collection as a result of gifts from me, and many have told me they saved the Cases, Hen & Roosters, Bucks, or Kissing Cranes for their grandchildren.

Customers also confided in me about their health problems. Men and women alike talked about their families, who sometimes became my friends as well.

I continue to remember favorite customers and miss their friendship and loyalty. Perhaps in all these small ways, my customers will not forget me.

Chapter 10
Learning, Loving, Laughing—Appalachian Language

I never made a mistake in grammar but one in my life and as soon as I done it I seen it.

—Carl Sandburg

America is rich in regional dialects, and, with the exception of Native Americans, we are a country of global immigrants. Each region has its own communication oddities. While I am not a student of linguistics, I find the dialect of southern Appalachia intriguing and unmatched.

My pastime during thirty-two years in outside sales was collecting pronunciations and idioms from customers and inhabitants in East Tennessee, Kentucky, Virginia, and West Virginia. I may have visited a company CEO in Knoxville, a school superintendent in Newport, a custodian in Pennington Gap, Virginia, or a police chief in Harlan, Kentucky. Wherever in southern Appalachia my customer lived, the dialect intrigued me.

"Appalachian speak" has been the subject of a wealth of books and articles. *Christy*, a 1967 novel by Catherine Marshall, documented the connection between Appalachian dialect and the English-Scottish immigrants to our southern mountains. A student of dialect would recognize Elizabethan influence in many mountain folks' words, for example, "yonder" as written by Shakespeare. Some wordsmiths insist this speech is ignorance or laziness, but I never thought of the people I met as stupid or slow.

> Instead of being called corrupt [it] ought to be classified as archaic. Many of the expressions heard throughout the region today can be found in the centuries-old words of some of the greatest English authors: Alfred, Chaucer, Shakespeare, and the men who contributed to the King James version of the Bible, to cite but a few (Dial 1969).

Regardless of the cause of double negatives (*I don't have nothin'),* an unnecessary "h" at the beginning of a word (*ain't* pronounced as *hain't*; *it* said as *hit*), incorrect tense (*I seen it; I done done it*), omission of the final "g" and / or addition of an "a" before verbs (*He's agoin' now*), and idioms too numerous to list, Appalachian speak is peculiar to outsiders. Rural Appalachia presented me with an abundance of material.

I soon learned, understood, and sometimes spoke the local dialect with my customers, and I didn't find typical Appalachian grammar or phonetics amusing. Humor came from customers' curious words, which I jotted in a confidential notebook during the years of meeting and greeting the folks in my territory. I never laughed aloud when a major mispronunciation occurred. "Edna Speak" filled many pages.

Edna, a chubby lunchroom lady whose hair changed monthly from black to brown or sometimes blond and brown, struck me as smart, efficient, and dedicated to her work, but she kept me chuckling privately. As she recounted her first trip to "Starback" (Starbucks), she fumed about the "Demy-toss" (demitasse). She took it to the barista for a refund because she refused to pay for her tiny cup of coffee.

When I complimented Edna on her office plant, a Wandering Jew, she bragged, "This is my new plant, a 'wondering' Jew." I silently chuckled, picturing the plant pondering:

Edna's co-workers and I happened on the subject of pancakes. A pancake gourmet, Edith said she wouldn't eat them unless she had Aunt Jemima syrup, which she called "Ann Jew Mama syrup."

Howard, a frail, balding, sanitation employee and chronic complainer, often whined about his fatigue, aches, and dizziness. On one of my visits, he appeared unusually cheerful. "They found my problem," he explained. "I went to a sleep study; my doctor diagnosed me with sleep acne." I'm sure he meant sleep *apnea*.

A police chief named Sherman ordered Fleet Wash from me. He suffered from "caramel" tunnel syndrome in his hands until he resorted to surgery. I wondered if he took ice cream to the operating room to go along with his tasty topping. Sherman sometimes needed tests at a nearby hospital, which suited him because the facility provided "ballet" parking. He usually ordered dinner from a local diner and often ordered "tater tics" (Tater Tots). Lunch was called dinner and dinner, supper in much of the rural South.

Lucille, a petite and attractive woman with an overbearing afro, worked as an assistant purchasing agent for a small city, ordering products for the maintenance crew. She requested a disinfectant, so I sold her one named Medaphene. The employees liked the product, so once a month Lucille called me.

"I need six cases of methamphetamine. The crew loves that stuff." I repeated the name correctly, but her pronunciation never changed. Each time she called my office phone to place her order, I expected a drug bust.

Howard, another customer and a country singer by night, city street supervisor by day, loved Dolly Parton, which was evident when he told me, "I saw that movie with Angelina Jolene (Jolie)." ("Jolene" is a song written and performed by Dolly Parton from her 1974 album, *Jolene.*) Howard had recently taken his grandchildren to see "Madagascard." As we talked about actresses, he mentioned that the hearing-impaired actor, Mary Matalin, one of his favorites, shouldn't have married James Carville. Surely he meant Marlee Matlin, the actor, and not the Republican political talking head, Mary Matalin, who is indeed married to Democratic strategist and pundit James Carville.

When my career in chemical sales was in its infancy, I called on a county highway department, determined to make a sale. I showed every product I could think of before noticing tar on all of the vehicles.

"We have an excellent tar remover," I began.

Henry, an ancient, tobacco-spitting mechanic, told me in his deep Tennessee drawl, "Honey, we have a man with a machine removes them tars." Tires.

Martha, an executive housekeeper, looked like what my father used to call pleasingly plump. The majority of the people I dealt with were plump—a polite way of saying overweight, and typical of folks who enjoy our southern cuisine.

Martha spoke loudly and often, usually about her wayward daughter, Shirley. Martha began telling a story about her child's latest transgression just as the girl phoned her. After hanging up, she exclaimed, "Shirley called me right as I mentioned her; she must have ESPN."

Henry, a young but balding maintenance supervisor for a large hospital, complained of a painful back injury as he explained his treatment. "I go to one of them choirpracters." I tried not to imagine doctors singing hymns to heal Henry.

Many times ordinary words emerged jumbled or mispronounced: Andouille sausage was "Hundoiey" sausage, perhaps a mixture of Hyundai cars and sausage. Water*millin*, a summertime fruit, was fun to take on a pic*neck*. And then there was General "Taco's" (Tso's) Chicken—the favorite Chinese dish for more than one customer.

Some customers explained that the "Rockwiller" is a scary dog that should be "spaded." Specific often emerged as "pacific," and fiscal year became "physical year." Wasps were pronounced "waspers," and the lovely iris (flower) turned into the "lovely Irish." More than one school principal took me to look at the new "Muriel" (mural) painted on a classroom wall.

Several of my business clients pronounced ear as "year." Most folks born and raised in this region have heard "r" or "t" added to simple words, like once (wunst), follow (foller), tomato (tomater, or simply, 'mater), and water (worter). The "o" ending on a word changes to "a," as in Ohio (Ohia), tobacco (tobacca), and tomato (tomada). My all-time favorite, though, is "you-uns" for ya'll.

Unique expressions dotted the southern mountains as well:

"You have fell off some." (You have lost weight.)

"He laid up in the bed." (He overslept.)

"Whatcha git fer it?" (How much does it cost?)

"The cat is up in under the table." (The cat is underneath the table.)

And, as I often heard from a reluctant buyer, "That product is high dollar stuff," or "Your chemicals are higher'n a cat's back." (Your product is expensive.)

Country people used the pronouns me, my, and you in unique ways. My clients often used the following sentence constructions:

"I am going out to smoke *me* a cigarette."

"I cook *my* pinto beans with fatback."

"Eat *you* one of them biscuits."

When a gentleman was upset at work, usually at his boss, he would declare, "I'll just go tahouse." (I will go to the house—meaning home.)

In addition to odd language, novel opinions on assorted subjects arose often. When the weather changed, you would get sick. Of course, if only one person became ill, this truism still held. For a chest cold, Vicks VapoRub worked best when you ate a spoonful, and green beans had to be cooked for several hours or you could be poisoned. You would also face a serious illness if fish and milk were eaten at the same meal. Not all customers held these notions, but enough did for me to make notes.

The words EYE-talian (Italian) MY-mosa (Mimosa) GIT-tar (Guitar) and FLAR-duh (Florida) echoed throughout my sales territory. A few examples of quirky speech, for sure, were "at" instead of that, "thu" instead of threw or through ("He thew 'at ball thu 'at winder), "'mere" for come here, and "itta" instead of it will.

I didn't see these friends and customers as dull; probably they simply spoke the way their parents, friends, and neighbors had spoken for decades. I discovered expressions I hadn't heard before, and they made my job a little more interesting. I'll give you one more amusing illustration. Freda, a wastewater plant supervisor and one of my earliest customers, purchased a drum of degreaser on my first visit. When I returned to check on the product, this customer, who was also an Evangelical Christian, waved our invoice for the herbicide at me.

"What kind of religion does your company represent?" Freda demanded. "This Amen Company is one I may not want to do business with."

I named my company Amann Industries because Amann is my birth name. Freda looked again at her invoice and realized her mistake. She became one of my best customers.

Amen.

Chapter 11
Wolves at the Door

I like to think of sales as the ability to gracefully persuade, not manipulate, a person or persons into a win-win situation.

—Bo Bennett, *Years to Success*

During my employment with the novelty and tobacco companies, I never felt the threat of competition from salespeople outside of the company. Supervisors and owners negotiated bids and prices with various stores. Snack food vendors often attempted to steal shelf space in groceries from each other, but the rivalry remained semi-friendly.

Food service vendors surprised me with the fierceness of their competition. Suggestions that women in sales swapped sex for business appalled customers who told about hearing these remarks from their salesmen. A sly salesperson sometimes retrieved my grocery supply company's invoices from the customers' desks. He then offered prices a few cents below mine in order to ensure business. Most buyers caught on to this trick and refused to purchase from these shysters.

Okay, I admit it. I did learn to read competitors' invoices upside down if they happened to be on a buyer's desk. But I never swiped any.

Cutthroat techniques in chemical sales seemed to be the norm. On my first day with the chemical company, colleagues warned me to keep my car locked at all times when with an account. Tales were told at sales meetings of representatives whose cars had been raided for customer lists. More than once, I noticed a competitor parked beside my car as I exited a business. One salesman followed me to Union County, TN, and back almost all the way to my home. Managers even cautioned me against putting old invoices in our outside garbage cans.

Trickery inflicted on unaware customers was on par with bribery, otherwise known as incentives. The old joke told to novice salespeople was that salesmen wore boots with a nail in the toe. They kicked the drum of product in the customer's warehouse, causing a leak. Later, they would return, shake the drum, and declare, "Hey, you're out of product. I'll send you some more right away."

Another trick involved dropping silver dollars into a barrel of chemical. When the barrel was empty, the dollars belonged to the customer. Supervisors often encouraged employees to work with chemicals from "dollar barrels," hyping the advantages of this superior product.

A super salesman I often encountered owned a condo in Florida. As his customers purchased a certain amount of product, they were treated to a week or two of vacation at his expense. Several salesmen took their best customers on golf and fishing trips. Extravagant rewards were beyond my means, so I treated most of my customers with pocketknives and lunches at local restaurants.

Boiler-room scams ran rampant among chemical and light bulb purveyors. One of my utility accounts ordered a large quality of degreaser from me every month. One day I visited the business and saw several drums of degreaser with labels different from mine.

"Wow, where did all this degreaser come from?" I questioned the purchasing agent, a good friend.

"Jake placed the order," she fumed. "He received pictures in the mail of a girl in a skimpy bikini. She called him the next day to say they were her photos. She was selling degreaser, so he ordered six 35-gallon drums from her." Wanda checked the invoice, and Bikini Babe's prices were more than double mine.

Boiler Room Scam Successful!

My Big Sale Stolen!

Local sales reps practiced fraudulent schemes, although rarely were they discovered, except by other representatives. When I first began my chemical sales career, supervisors were not the only ones who purchased products. Other employees ordered merchandise, and devious sales reps were aware of this fact. I often noticed cases and drums of products in an account and wondered who'd ordered them.

"Old Joe must have bought these before he retired." I'd heard these similar words too often and knew Old Joe did not place that order. Many times when an employee retired, quit, or was fired, case after case of chemicals and light bulbs arrived, and no one knew who ordered them.

Often an office employee received a phone call from an unfamiliar salesperson, requesting a purchase order number. "Henry needed a barrel of herbicide and told me to get a purchase order." *Not true!*

"Henry no longer works here, but I'll give you the P.O. number."

"We don't need this drum of floor cleaner, but I guess we'll keep it since Frank ordered it before he left."

"It costs too much freight to return it," the discussion would go.

I would argue that by simply refusing it, some of the dishonesty might stop, but usually folks didn't want the hassle and paid the invoice.

One of the brashest salesmen I encountered appeared to control his own accounts and order whatever he pleased. Duane's method was to offer his services to a business by maintaining inventories. He replaced products like wall deodorizers, urinal screens, hand cleaners, and other items as needed. He was "saving the custodian the trouble" of installing and refilling equipment.

I watched as he counted stock in a warehouse. He then emptied all the products on the shelves into a crate he carried with him, took it out to his car, and drove away. Now he was able to reorder chemicals. I thought about complaining to my customer, but I figured he would think sour grapes. The salesman was later caught throwing chemicals in a dumpster outside of an industrial account.

One account purchased hand soap dispensers from me, which I installed in every restroom. On my next visit, I discovered the hand dispensers in a trash can. A custodian complained, "That salesman came in here, and when he saw your dispensers, he took them off the wall and threw them in the garbage. I told my boss, and he banned the man from our business." For once, the jerk was thwarted.

Of course, these dishonest people were the exceptions. And as buyers became more aware of scammers, honest sales reps sold more products and developed loyal customers. Most people in business are not interested in extravagant gifts. They are concerned about the quality of products and the ethics of the seller, and they expect a salesperson to care genuinely about them and their business.

Chapter 12
Rub-A-Dub-Dub, Suds and Bleach in the Tub

Not all chemicals are bad. Without chemicals such as hydrogen and oxygen, for example, there would be no way to make water, a vital ingredient in beer.

—Dave Barry

If cleanliness is next to godliness, then bleach must be holy water, and suds are surely sacrosanct. The reverence my customers held for bleach and suds remains a mystery to me.

Fetid chlorine assaulted my nose at nearly every account. School custodians tossed gallons of bleach on the walls and floors of children's bathrooms. Daycare facilities emitted the foul, toxic fumes from playrooms and babies' sleeping areas alike, seemingly without any awareness of danger. Many small healthcare facilities cleaned air-conditioning units with chlorine bleach, sending the noxious fumes throughout patients' rooms

Chlorine contains dioxin, designated a carcinogen by the American Public Health Association in Washington, D.C. I worked with employees who insisted on using chlorine as a floor cleaner, deodorizer, and even air spray without diluting the chemical. During my years in chemical sales, I conducted safety seminars, instructional floor-care meetings, Material Safety Data training sessions, and several cleaning and safety courses.

Inhalation of small concentrations of chlorine irritates the nose and throat and can cause headaches. Intermediate amounts of chlorine may immediately cause chest pain, nausea, vomiting, coughing, and shortness of breath, the American Academy of Pediatrics and the American Heart Association remind us.

During my sales tenure, chlorine bleach became the focus of more than one training class. The chemical is a severe respiratory irritant and can give off a toxic gas when mixed with other products, especially ammonia. But mix it many employees did.

"Bleach destroys germs and smells nice."

"I use bleach to deodorize my house. I love the fresh smell."

"I add bleach to my dish*worshing* powders."

"Baby nurseries must be sprayed with bleach every day." Yes, soak the toys in a mixture of bleach and water, letting them dry thoroughly before returning them to children's areas. But many women insisted on spraying concentrated bleach in every room.

One nursing home laundry assistant questioned me when I related that I seldom used bleach.

"You don't bleach your underwear? Goodness me, I'd be afraid to wear underpants that ain't been bleached!" Other employees concurred.

"Them germs you pick up from toilet seats!"

Customers reacted to the denunciation of chlorine as though I had ridiculed their favorite child, but I was determined to replace bleach with a safer product. I eventually found that chemical and rushed to tell every customer.

After starting my company, I attended a chemical industry trade show in Chicago where I learned that one of our suppliers had discovered a way to stabilize hydrogen peroxide, add a pleasant fragrance, and market it. The chemist designed this Environmental Protection Agency-registered product to replace bleach and other disinfectants, but prying bleach from the lunchroom cook's dishpan hands proved difficult, if not impossible.

The hydrogen peroxide based product, H2Orange2, touted safe use on more surfaces than did chlorine. The neutral product emitted no toxic fumes and didn't irritate hands or eyes. At first, customers complained about the new products' price, telling me bleach cost about a dollar per gallon. But after the recommended dilution of 128 parts water to 1 part H2Orange2, the cost of this hydrogen peroxide product dropped to roughly twenty cents per gallon.

After providing a multitude of personal demonstrations across my territory, I managed to convince most hands-on employees to accept this safer chemical. H2Orange2 became my number one product. The Federal Occupational Safety and Health Administration (OSHA) helped my safety measures with its demands for MSDS on all products used in the workplace. MSDS are Material Safety Data Sheets, or as suppliers and customers alike called them, "MSDS Sheets" (a redundancy translating to Material Safety Data Sheet sheets).

In 1986, industries began requiring all departments to comply with OSHA standards. Still, it would take several years and multiple fines for municipalities to become fully OSHA compliant.

A poster in an industrial maintenance office read: *If You Think OSHA Is a Small Town in Ohio, You May Be in Trouble.* In fact, employers who ignored the MSDS requirements could face fines of up to $10,000 per day per incident. Still, even with hefty fines, many schools systems and municipalities I visited were reluctant to hold the classes required to teach employees why they needed to learn about the safety material. Industrial customers were quick to offer safety training, but educational facilities were the last to begin requiring MSDS.

I learned everything I could about the new government rulings, conducting MSDS seminars for interested customers. Slowly, the safety data sheets became standard, and copies became available for anyone in any industry.

Before these rulings, hazardous chemicals were abundant in the workplaces I visited. For instance, it wasn't unusual for vehicle repair garages to keep an open drum of gasoline for hand washing; mechanics even used it as a floor cleaner. The dangerous solvent 111-trichloroethane (methyl chloroform) appeared in garages and air-conditioning repair shops alike. The

EPA and OSHA finally outlawed many of these chemicals, though bleach may still be used if safety protection is provided when disinfecting with chlorine.

Soapsuds rivaled bleach in terms of customer demand. I learned to sell liquid laundry soap when customers asked for "worshun' powders," but employees insisted the soap must produce suds. According to Dawn's Dishwashing Liquid website, suds do not clean. Surfactants (cleaning agents) do the dirty work. My customers wanted sudsy water in the sinks, regardless.

During the years my company held a bid with a county school food-service system, problems arose. I usually solved them. Cafeteria managers and cooks seemed receptive to suggestions and willing to try what I recommended, but they refused to relinquish dreaded *bleach* and the always-popular *suds.*

My supplier of pot-and-pan soap, used by school cafeterias for hand-sink cleaning agents, formulated the soap to the specs I requested, but a few women complained, "Your soap doesn't have enough suds to clean our pots and pans." The pots looked clean to me, but I saw no point in arguing. The customer is always right.

Pot and pan soap dispenser

When school lunchroom cooks wanted more suds, our chemist instructed his warehouse team to simply add a sudsing formula to the soap. As with the pink deodorizer for Brushy Mountain prison, the soap worked perfectly once it contained additional suds. Behold, a fountain of suds erupted, and lo, the pots were clean.

During the early 2000s, customers became more concerned with personal safety and environmental hazards caused by harsh chemicals. As companies began to develop safer, "greener" products, bleach became less in demand as an all-purpose cleaner and deodorizer. In fact, many school systems have now restricted the use of bleach as a cleaning agent. Once more, new ideas, environmental awareness, safety measures, and the misuse of hazardous chemicals came to assist my sales career.

Blood-borne pathogen rulings offered me an opportunity to present seminars and expand my product line to include personal protections-gloves, protective suits and eyewear, disinfectants, and body fluid cleanup items. Ergonomic workplace studies provided lines of products ranging from back-support belts for employees lifting heavy objects to ergonomic training videos.

HIV remained a dreaded disease, but other more prevalent, life-threatening infections such as Hepatitis C and MRSA (methicillin-resistant Staphylococcus aureus) presented opportunities for increasing my product lines. They also provided occasions to educate my customers about self-protection.

MRSA is a bacterium that causes infections in different parts of the body. It's tougher to treat than most strains of staph because it's extremely resistant to many commonly prescribed antibiotics. According to the Mayo Clinic website (www.mayoclinic.com), it is spread by skin-to-skin contact, and particularly at-risk populations include high-school wrestlers, childcare workers, and people living in crowded conditions.

A few of my customers mentioned knowing of someone with MRSA, but I found it virtually impossible to convince anyone of the advantages of a disinfectant which destroyed 99.99 percent of the deadly bacteria on hard surfaces. The answer I frequently heard was, "I never heard of the disease, but if we get an epidemic, I'll order some of that disinfectant." *By then you may be too late,* I often thought and sometimes advised.

I spent days calling on high school and college coaches and daycare workers only to be told, "MRSA? Don't know what it is. Nope, we don't need your disinfectant. We keep our school / jail / daycare clean."

Or, "I'm not worried about it, but I'll let you know if we hear of an outbreak." "We just spray bleach—chlorine will kill anything." These were memorable instances when I failed to convince many customers of a product that should have been an absolute necessity in every account.

Martha, a public housing apartment manager in Knoxville, eagerly listened to my disinfectant presentation and thoroughly read the literature I presented.

"My niece recently gave birth. Both she and her baby contracted MRSA in the hospital," Martha said, nearly in tears. She described their horrible illness. She also knew this disease to be extremely contagious. I suggested Martha order this product for cleaning the units, as I knew she had purchasing power.

"We'll try bleach first, and if it doesn't work, I'll order some of your chemical. Before you go, will you give me a gallon as a sample?" I didn't give her a sample nor did I visit the complex again.

My greatest concern, as with employees mixing chlorine with other chemicals, was for the health and safety of those in the workplace. My new mission during this time period? I would convince customers to purchase EPA-registered antimicrobial products for cleaning and disinfecting.

I am pleased with the widespread use of safer chemicals today. Our environment is somewhat more protected. I wonder why the changes didn't occur thirty years earlier when bleach ranked among my stiffest competitors.

The Top Ten List of How You Can Tell if Your OSHA Inspection Is Going Poorly

10. OSHA sets up temporary housing in your company parking lot.
9. The compliance officer mutters, "This is unbelievable" each time he or she enters a different department.
8. OSHA calls in a professional film crew to document conditions at your company, and a reporter from *Dateline* tags along.

7. The compliance officer insists on wearing a moon suit supplied with SCBA (self-contained breathing apparatus,) while employees continue to work in jeans and tennis shoes.

6. The congressman you called for help won't return your call, but he does return your campaign contribution.

5. The compliance office begins the opening conference with, "You have the right to remain silent."

4. The compliance officer asks you a specific question about a report in your files, but you haven't turned over any files.

3. The compliance officer knows each of your employees by his or her first name.

2. The compliance officer is a former employee that you fired.

1. The current OSHA president conducts the closing conference.

Original source: *Maintenance Supplies Magazine,* August 2005
www.hsegroup.com

Chapter 13
I Know Every Restroom in Every Town

(Apologies to Roger Miller)

I listen like mad to any conversation taking place next to me just trying to hear why this is funny. Women's restrooms are especially great.

—Lynda Barry, American cartoonist and author

Sixty thousand is the approximate number of times I have needed to find a public restroom during thirty-two years selling various products on the road, oftentimes in a town too small to support McDonalds or Hardees or other fast food eateries. Even in larger towns, chain restaurants were not always present in the '80s and '90s. Locating a clean stall presented a constant and demanding challenge. I took a chance that any restroom I found would be sanitary, and I also knew I should carefully check the toilet seat in a ladies restroom before sitting.

Jesus is coming! R U Ready? Pamphlets appeared in dozens of restrooms. *Who puts them in stalls? The Holy Ghost?* These pamphlets gave me an idea because women often pee on public toilet seats. Disgusting!

For vengeance, I printed my own signs: *$50 Fine for Peeing on Toilet Seat!* I carried Scotch tape in my purse and taped the signs to the inside doors of bathroom stalls when using a public restroom. This little flyer made me smile when I thought of a squatter reading my warning. The Pee on Seat custom baffles me. Wet toilet seats dredged up memories of my childhood, my grandmother, and the Saturdays we spent together.

During my childhood, restrooms contained a dispenser where you cranked a germy handle to receive a clean patch of cloth towel for hand drying. Numerous women used the bars of iodine-scented soap provided, bacteria skulking in the suds.

Grandmother and I often spent Saturdays in downtown Knoxville, eating lunch at the old S&W Cafeteria and taking in a movie. Like most children, I often needed to use a restroom, and Grandmother insisted I put toilet paper on a seat before sitting. She panicked at the idea of germs lurking there to assault me, but she never told me to wet on the seat. In truth, more germs are likely found on faucets, door handles, and light switches than on toilet seats.

According to research at the United Kingdom's Charted Society of Physiotherapy (whew!), squatting to avoid contact with a toilet seat can increase the incidence of urinary tract infections by preventing the bladder from emptying completely. A large percent of women seem unaware of this fact. They refuse to sit on a toilet seat instead of carefully lining the seat with adequate toilet tissue.

This paper-on-seat theory resulted in an embarrassing situation during my sales career. I had finally purchased a business suit (half-price) of the type I'd coveted since my early sales years. I wore it to make introductory calls on several purchasing departments of the largest industry in Oak Ridge, TN: Oak Ridge National Laboratory. After completing the necessary forms to visit a multitude of buyers, I used the restroom, which was clean, I might add. Afterward, I waited in the reception area and then walked down hallways to speak with several buyers. My business finished, I walked to my car, located across a vast parking area. As I pulled out of the parking space, a strange woman yelled and raised her hands as she ran towards me.

"Is she crazy?" I wondered, as I cracked my window to ask what she wanted.

"I just had to catch you," she panted. "I noticed you as you walked down the hallway. Sheets of toilet paper are draped from your skirt to your shoes."

"Thank you," I replied. *And gee, thank you, Grandmother.*

Restrooms today have changed dramatically from my childhood days. Many toilet areas install seat cover dispensers (although they're often empty), electric hand dryers, toilet paper dispensers (some only a contortionist could reach), and, best of all, No Touch soap and paper towel dispensers.

A British university study found that hand dryers in public restrooms harbor more harmful bacteria, including feces, than any restroom surface. Paper towels are the most sanitary way to dry hands. I consider hand sanitizer a miracle product that became one of my best-selling items soon after its introduction and before it became readily available over the counter. School principals purchased hand sanitizer and gave a bottle to each teacher. Surprisingly, I sold the greatest amount of the sanitizer to utility employees and street crew workers. These folks mostly packed their lunches and ate in company trucks with no opportunity to wash their hands before eating.

Pungent and unpleasant odors of urine, feces, vomit, and even sewer gas are another source of discomfort in public restrooms, according to *Sanitary Maintenance Magazine.* Patrons expect or at least hope to be greeted by a pleasant or neutral fragrance when they enter these areas. Sometimes custodians are instructed to spray or dispense via wall-mounted dispensers an odor-control product that may simply mask odors. When I visited a customer's restroom facilities to suggest deodorizing products, a neutral scent to counteract smells was my choice. I discouraged custodians from purchasing a fragrant deodorizer for public restrooms because perfumed smells may trigger asthma attacks.

"Thorough cleaning of urinals and floor grout, both harbingers of dirt and bacteria, helps to eliminate malodor," states *Sanitary Maintenance Magazine* (March 2009). I demonstrated an enzyme and/or disinfectant, rather than strong chlorine or ammoniated cleaner. I discouraged using bleach as a cleaner and deodorizer. The chlorine odor also may cause asthma attacks. Chlorine is extremely dangerous to employees whose jobs include cleaning restrooms.

Over many years, I became skilled at locating someplace to "go." Never use a service station toilet located outside the building—they are typically not clean. Women's restrooms have the most graffiti: "Trixie is a Whore," "Lester Luvs Me," and "Frankie ❤ Johnnie" are but a few. Men's toilet areas often smell strongly of urine and generally have no toilet paper. I know, because I have entered hundreds of men's restrooms to demonstrate urinal blocks, flush valve cleaner, and drain opener.

I have, indeed, found the most routinely clean and well-stocked restrooms for both men and women. If the town is the county seat, use the courthouse or find the utility company. No one will question you if you carry a clipboard or briefcase. City hall or any municipality with women employees will usually have clean restrooms. They usually are furnished with bathroom tissue, paper towels, and perhaps an air freshener. Most women who work in offices insist on cleanliness for their personal business.

Today, many fast-food eateries have clean and accessible restrooms. State rest areas, always clean and well stocked, are also a welcome sight for a needy traveler. Unfortunately, when I was traveling, most of my driving took place in mountain towns far away from interstates with their pleasant restrooms.

Oddly, the dirtiest and most lacking in necessities are frequently the toilet areas in grocery and smaller department stores. One grocery I frequented kept the same fly strip, dotted with its long-dead prey, for many years.

A restaurant famous for its buffet slopped around a dirty mop dipped in filthy water, seemingly never changed, to clean bathroom floors.

During my travels, I have never encountered a female manager or supervisor of a restaurant, grocery store, or department store, so public restroom facilities at those places remained questionable at best. It would be helpful if the man in charge of a facility asked a wife, daughter, or female employee to inspect the toilet area to ensure that it's sanitary, appropriately designed, and properly supplied.

1. Toilet paper dispensers should be full.

2. Purse hangers need to be mounted on the inside of stall doors within reach.

3. Toilet paper should turn loosely on holders. Nobody wants to wipe her ass with confetti!

4. Hand soap dispensers should be full, and the soap should not be diluted in order to save money.

5. Floors and toilet or urinal areas should be cleaned daily.

Companies that purchase 1-ply toilet paper to save money are actually spending more than if they bought 2-ply. Buying 2-ply toilet paper results in less floor clutter, making the restroom cleaning crews' job easier and faster. With 1-ply, people tear many more pieces off the roll, trying to grab a section long enough to do the job. Countless facilities dilute hand-dispenser soap with water to cut costs. This miserly practice causes waste from dripping hand soap, which doesn't clean as well.

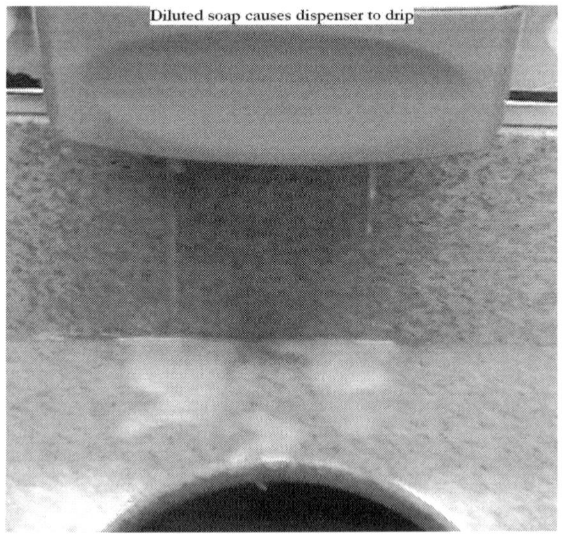
Diluted soap causes dispenser to drip

Overall, state rest areas boast the cleanest, most well-stocked restrooms, though they are sometimes many miles apart. If you spot that rest area sign while on the road, stop and "go." Otherwise you may have to tinkle down the way at a service station where the attendant hands you a greasy key dangling from a dirty stick and points you to a menacing door around back by the dumpsters. And don't forget your hand sanitizer.

Chapter 14
Cuisine in the Country

If you're going to America, bring your own food.

—Fran Lebowitz

In a time before the Cracker Barreling of most major interstate exits in the south and Burger Kingdoms ruling in small towns, lunch places were difficult to find on my sales routes.

Many restaurants amused me with menu choices, posters, or attitudes. Mom and Pop "Kuntry Kitchens" were usually the only places for cheap eats and often displayed unique menus.

Mom and Pop eateries inhabited smaller towns, while "The Steak House," as my customers called any restaurant that served grilled beef and baked potatoes, was found in larger areas. Western Sizzler, Ryan's, no matter the name, they called it "The Steak House." Customers considered it a fancy place to eat for birthdays or anniversaries. Smaller café owners cleverly named their businesses "Kuntry Kitchen," "Kuntry Kookin'" or some other variation of "country."

A little restaurant in Jacksboro, TN, posted daily specials on a chalk-board. I dined at this café each month. On the menu board, along with the expected meat and two vegetables, the owner always displayed "peas" in quotation marks:

Roast beef with au jus gravy (or sometimes simply "roast beef with au jus dipping sauce")

Mashed potatoes with gravy

Pole beans

Jell-O

"Peas"

More curious menu sightings were the "vegetable" offerings in other country kitchens:

Broccoli (cooked until it turned a pale greenish yellow), served with Velveeta cheese sauce

Macaroni and Velveeta cheese sauce and/or Cheez Whiz

Peaches and cottage cheese

Fruit cup with Jell-O

Pickled eggs

Grits

Turkey dressing

Soup du jour of the day (Translation: "Soup of the day" of the day)

Clam Chowder soup (In other words, clam soup soup)

No matter what the side dish offering, the restaurant called it a "vegetable."

A curious poster in a pancake restaurant issued a warning: ***"Shoes and Shirts Must Be Worn to Be Served."*** I wondered how many shoes and shirts unaccompanied by a person had attempted to enter the restaurant.

Meat was a star attraction in country cuisine, but I soon became tired of pale, overcooked cube steak, greasy fried chicken, and lumpy meatloaf. Perhaps I became a vegetarian as a result of too much unappetizing meat. However, vegetarianism, when dining in the country, proved daunting.

Green beans, pintos, cabbage, and even Brussels sprouts contained tiny bites of ham in every serving. I once ordered cornbread and took a bite before complaining to the waitress, "This cornbread has brittle, crunchy things in it."

"Them's cracklins," the porky country waitress patiently explained. She looked as if she had eaten more than her share of country cooking. "Them's hog cracklins."

How silly of me.

Vegetable soup arrived with chunks of unidentifiable meat. Cooks smothered mashed potatoes in meat gravy even if I ordered them without. If I sent them back, waitresses simply scraped off the offending goo, again presenting them with a smile and a "Here you go, Honey."

Iced tea, our "Chablis of the South," was drunk heartily with each country meal. It would be sweet—cloyingly sweet. It should have been served with a Karo syrup sticker on the glass. Order it unsweetened, and you invited a puzzled frown from your waitress. No matter the time of day, coffee cups were present with your place setting, and your server came by with a coffee pot. Was this practice of drinking coffee with lunch and dinner only found in the South?

I located some pleasant restaurants along my routes that offered fruit salads, peanut butter sandwiches, and other non-meat fare. Mildred's Diner in Wartburg, TN, which featured "The Famous Wartburger," also served fruit plates and meat-free vegetables.

My favorite small café placed a sign in its window:

We can seat 1000 people—28 at a time.

COUNTRY COOKING
LUNCH 11 AM-2PM
CREASY GREENS
TURNIPS
SWEET POTATO
APPLES
CIDER

Chapter 15
Retrograde Retirement

So many roads, so many roads
So many roads I know
All I want is one to take me home

—Robert Hunter, Grateful Dead

Thirteen years filled with excitement, education, and effort while operating my company were coming to an end in 2007. Freight fees increased dramatically as trucking companies, UPS, and Fed Ex added fuel surcharges on top of freight costs. Manufacturers' costs of goods escalated, and suppliers demanded minimum orders on all products, forcing me to buy in excess of customer needs.

Cash flow soon restricted my ability to accept special requests from customers as more and more suppliers demanded a minimum order from my company. Many vendors requested a 36-case purchase order when my customer needed only one or two. As gas prices rose, I could no longer justify driving to counties miles away in hopes of making even a small sale.

Some of my most profitable citrus-based products contained d-limonene, produced from an orange peel extract. As customers desired more natural green products, orange prices increased fourfold. In many cases, the cost to my customers of Big Orange, Orange Lady, drain degreaser, and a host of other products became prohibitive.

Walmarts and Sam's Clubs multiplied in East Tennessee like nature's little helicopters that rain from maple trees in springtime—without the charm. As if on cue, municipalities hired purchasing agents determined to save money. Buyers surmised that company costs could be dramatically reduced if mechanics and custodians bought the bulk of their products at Big Box stores. Whether this was true or not, I lost a tremendous amount of business. Another phenomenon I call Outsource Epidemic seized a significant part of my business.

A snail and a turtle crashed into each other at a stop sign. The officer who was called to the scene inquired of the snail the nature of the accident. The snail replied, "I don't know officer, it all happened so fast!"

My customers and I felt like the snail when outsourcing abruptly resulted in the dismissal of many employees. Government housing and educational facilities began hiring outside maintenance or cleaning services. Upper management or governing boards of utility departments opted to use outside companies for grounds-keeping services, displacing a large number of employees. The thinking was that institutions could save wages, eliminate employee health insurance, halt workers compensation, and trim expenses for products that they purchased.

During my years in sales, I often witnessed elected officials, appointed municipal managers, and school system administrators weighing short-term savings over future consequences. Simply put, they hoped to save money by cutting essential upgrades and repairs.

Schools I had visited for twenty or more years traditionally employed longtime custodians who represented a large part of school staff. These men and women cared for the school. They performed duties that went beyond cleaning. Without exception, scores of custodians I have worked with insisted on proper products to clean buildings and maintain floors. When school employees were fired in favor of a cleaning service, the quality of cleaning diminished.

"Our floors are ruined because outsource employees used inferior products," custodians at more than one school complained, when service companies' contracts expired and in-house custodians returned.

"Stainless steel fixtures and drinking fountains are tarnished. They cleaned with a cheap acid," Gwen, environmental supervisor at a Loudon County, TN country club, moaned. Outsource companies had to purchase cheaper and often inferior products in order to make a larger profit.

School-bus garage workers as well as city and county vehicle mechanics knew each vehicle in their facility. The men maintained detailed records showing which grease worked best. They proved that purchasing more expensive, yet better quality gear oil, grease, or hydraulic fluid led to lower expenses because automotive parts simply lasted longer. Management began to insist that garage employees order the cheapest grease, and sometimes repairs were even outsourced to local garages.

Over time, a city manager in KY explained, "Our costs have doubled since we outsourced repairs, but our council members still believe they're saving money."

A large government housing facility employed several in-house plumbers who purchased drain products from me and other suppliers. This facility oversaw hundreds of housing units. Their plumbers could race to solve drain problems within a few minutes. An air conditioning repair squad stayed active as well. They ordered several AC products from me. On one particular visit, the foreman called me into his office.

"Management has decided to outsource plumbing and air-conditioning maintenance. All the guys except me have been dismissed. How can a commercial plumber or AC company that charges by the hour possibly replace my men?" I wondered, too, and knew I would lose a large part of my sales.

These factors, along with my advancing age and joyful times spent with Estella, my first granddaughter, were causing me to question my company's future. After much soul searching, I realized retirement offered my only viable solution.

My remaining loyal customers purchased practically all of their products from me and asked me to locate a new supplier. I had learned from my years of experience in chemical sales about scamming and boiler room phone calls that would send my customers unwanted, unneeded, and expensive merchandise. I knew of a local chemical supplier with a decent reputation whose reps were some of my competitors. Putting aside my pride, I called the company. As much as it pained me, I offered competitors my customer lists. "Let me take you to lunch," offered the company owner, "and we'll discuss your proposal." Beverly, the company's sales manager asked snidely when we met, "We think you might be planning a con." No, I merely loved my customers and hoped they would receive honest and careful attention from vendors.

Retirement, even with the intermittent delight of Estella, plunged me into periods of boredom and inactivity. I missed my customers, especially when the company that took my accounts called me often with questions about products I had sold to those customers. And an income deficiency added tarnish to retirement pleasures.

After a year and a half of idleness, my competitors asked me to join them. They promised that my old buyers would be mine again. Without hesitating, I said yes and signed a non-compete agreement. The manager handed me a customer list with most of the names marked through, telling me he had already assigned my customers to family sales reps in his family-owned company.

Without my best accounts, they expected me to write orders by opening new business. I expressed disappointment, but I should have expected this after my experiences with other sales companies. After all, I *had* given them my business contacts. As little more than a year had passed, I approached Mr. Sam, "I really didn't plan on cold-calling most days. My best customers have phoned and asked me to be their rep again." He refused my request.

I kept a few people to sell to while I opened more accounts. Company policy allowed me to keep the few accounts that had never purchased from them. My new employer paid a fair commission and sent our commission checks each week, which was unusual for a chemical company. Working kept me occupied. Sales provided a decent income. After nearly three more years in sales, I was tired—tired of driving in rain, heat, and cold, tired of people, tired of making polite conservation—simply tired. I stayed with the company two and a half years until I couldn't make myself drive another day to *Rogers*ville, *James*town, *Friend*sville, *Mary*ville, *Helen*wood, *John*son City, *Jeff*erson City or any other town that had been my friend on the road for more than thirty years.

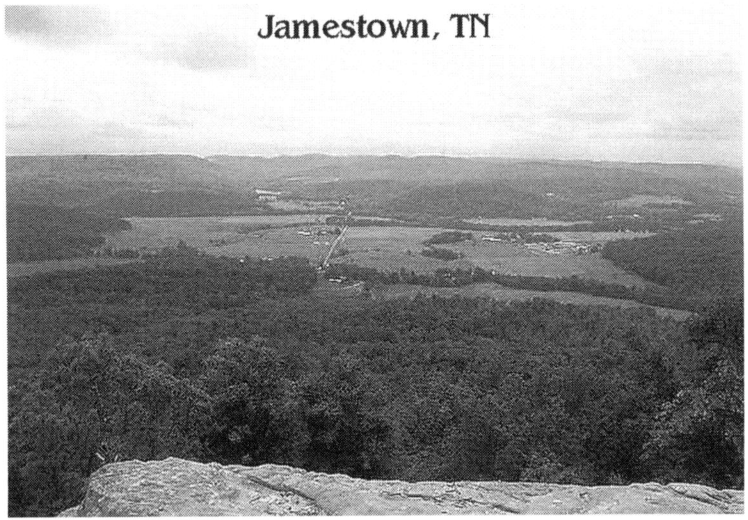

Chapter 16
I've Come to the End of My Appalachian Journey

My whole thesis is that you can't understand America until you understand Appalachia.

—Jeff Biggers, American author and journalist

As I count the 1,200,000 miles I've driven in thirty-two years of outside selling, I ponder my sales career. Should I have chosen a position with benefits, similar to the one offered by the University of Tennessee that would have been more secure and offered health insurance and retirement perks?

I cherish the wild and exciting adventures of traveling alone to picturesque and often frightening regions of southern Appalachia, seeing beauty as well as poverty along the way.

No town in our country is more breathtaking than Tellico Plains, TN, and no drive more scenic than from Tellico Plains to Cleveland, TN, where I detoured to Ocoee Scenic River State Park. Seeking customers and picturesque vistas, I drove from Chattanooga to Copper Hill, TN. Copper Hill offered a startling vision of coppery skeletons. Located in Polk County, it was once a thriving copper-mining town until fumes from smelting copper destroyed vegetation and eroded the land. Still, Polk County enchanted me each time I passed through searching for customers.

Copper Mines, circa 1939

Few folks I met had been to or heard of Stony Fork in Caryville, TN, perched atop a treacherous mountain. I, terrified, proudly reached the town of one school with only three students in its senior class.

I valued the Tennessee route from Wartburg to Jamestown, along Pilot Mountain, passing though the historic Victorian village of Rugby. Often, I changed my schedule so I could pass through Sunbright, TN, because the name made me smile. Obed Wild and Scenic River, Frozen Head State Park, and the Great Smoky Mountains found me searching for maintenance crews who purchased disinfectants and deodorizers for Porta-Potties, hand sanitizer, and insecticides.

In 1996, Atlanta hosted the summer Olympics and Ocoee River held a Whitewater Rafting event. Cheerfully, I drove along the route and met several park rangers who let me watch the construction until security detail blocked the road. And that's the closest I will ever get to an Olympic event.

Driving from Dandridge, TN, across Douglas Lake and into Sevierville, I found maintenance customers at Douglas Dam. Roads from Newport to Gatlinburg displayed beauty to behold. My mother told me Newport, once known as Bloody Newport, might be a dangerous town to visit and perhaps I shouldn't go there. Her warnings only made me more excited about visiting this mountain city.

On one frequent journey, I drove from Tazewell, through White Pine, and into Cocke County, along the French Broad River. In Newport, nestled in surrounding mountains, and along the Pigeon River, I established

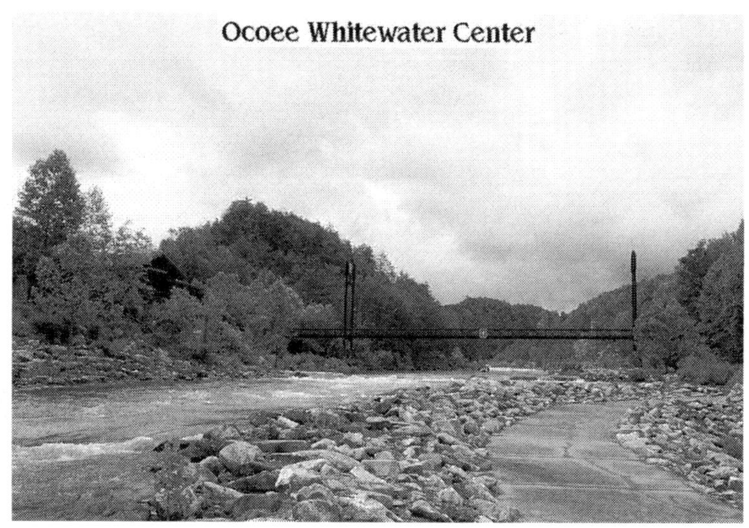
Ocoee Whitewater Center

numerous accounts and found the residents kind and willing to let me demonstrate my products.

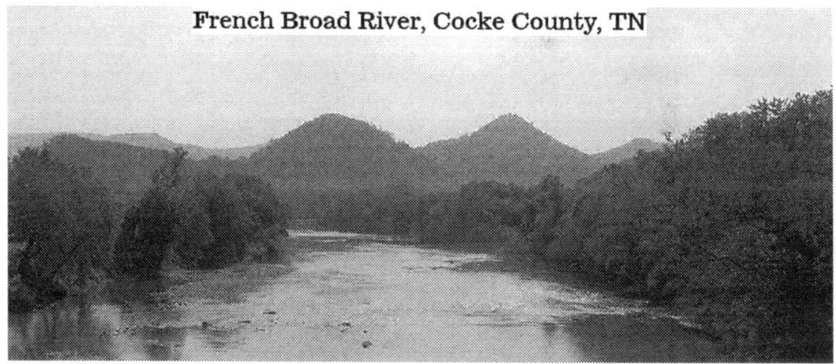
French Broad River, Cocke County, TN

Mechanics at the Cocke County Department of Education Bus Garage came to my rescue after I pulled up to the only drive-up pay phone in town. I neglected to turn off the car lights, and as I finished my many phone calls, a dead battery mocked me. Luckily, I found another twenty-five cents and soon Charlie from the bus garage arrived to charge my car's battery.

The route from Knoxville to historical Rogersville, TN, carried me along scenic Cherokee Lake. Campbell County, an area I visited frequently, boasted serene Cove Lake. Both waters provided fishing sites. I often packed my rod and reel with me on these trips, stopping to fish and hike on my way home.

Frozen Head State Park in Morgan County, situated in the Cumberland Mountains of East Tennessee, offered a tranquil area to enjoy my picnic lunch after visiting the park ranger for his chemical order.

In earlier years of my sales career, trips to Big Stone Gap, VA, Williamson, West VA, Harlan or Hazard, KY, and Jonesboro, TN, provided me with landscapes I'd never imagined as I drove along by myself, deciding which way to travel. One route took me from Knoxville to Banner Elk, NC, where I marveled at the quiet beauty of Cherokee National Forest.

Cherokee National Forest

Sneedville, TN, population 1,300 or so, turned out to be a town with nary a visiting sales rep. When I drove from Tazewell via Washburn, I realized why. The beauty of the Clinch River characterized this quaint little town, but only one road led into and out of the county. Customers purchased from me often, and I loved driving throughout Hancock County.

I valued the companionship of each small town as well as the people who lived in them. Friendsville's name seemed fitting because in the first school I visited, I received an order for chemicals. The principal sent me to the fire chief, who called a coal company owner on my behalf, who sent me to the county highway department. This charmed chain of events continued in most counties that befriended me until I not only knew "every restroom in every town," and each lunch spot, but also supervisors, road crews, city managers, and a list of folks too numerous to name.

A favorite town, Helenwood, gave me my first lumber company customer. Fred invited me into his office, ordered a case of grease, and inquired, "Want to know how Helenwood got her name?"

"Sure," I said, anxious to learn some history.

"Well," Fred began, "them army boys come thu here ridin' a train. They was two sisters, names of Helen and Shirley them boys was acourtin'. But they all wanted Helen, cause Shirley wouldn't, but Helen would. That's how come it's called Helenwood," laughed Fred.

Tourist destinations abound in Tennessee, Virginia, Kentucky, West Virginia, and North Carolina, but genuine glorious discoveries lie in the untraveled back roads and mountains in southern Appalachia. Memories of hundreds of customers who purchased from me and became friends are now an indelible part of me.

Tim, school transportation supervisor in Roane County, TN, brightened my day each time I visited. He told me about other sales reps who visited him and pranks he and his staff pulled. His crew often opened the hood of a visiting salesman's car and left an open can of sardines on the engine. Whenever the school systems hired a new secretary, a surprise greeted her. No, not flowers. Tim and his crew arrived early to turn all her file cabinets and desk to face the walls. A new school superintendent walked into his office only to find his desk, chair, and all other furniture, including pictures, in the restroom.

Jackie Teague, Matt Russell, Tim Goss

I fondly think of Nona, manager of a HUD apartment, whose baby girl Callie was born with cerebral palsy. Callie always offered me a sweet smile; she turned thirty when I retired. Gene, a gentlemanly custodian, always welcomed me no matter how busy he was with his chores. His concern for students and faculty alike showed when he asked for quality products to keep his school clean and polished. I think of New Market School in Jefferson County, TN, whose staff became good friends and whose principal, Mr. Strange, wanted the best possible products for his school.

So many different and unique folks I met, and I only wish I'd had the foresight to take photos of them. Many customers that I knew have retired or passed away, making room for younger buyers and sharper sales reps.

Sales reps that I encounter today with their rolling sample cases, laptops, smart phones, and iPads are fortunate to have the newest materials. Because of global positioning systems in company cars, these salespeople don't get lost the way I did. Their companies enjoy social media that promotes the merchandise they sell. Salesmen and saleswomen alike have the advantage of texting or e-mailing customers for appointments and sending pictures of new products. Would any of them want a sales career with untrustworthy vehicles, out-of-date road maps, and phantom phone booths? Perhaps not, but when I see them hurry into appointments or stock their products on grocery shelves, I long to tell them about my experiences.

Gary Strange, former principal New Market School
New Market, TN

No other profession could have shown me how a wastewater plant operates or taken me to rock crushers, landfills, and coal mines to sell grease. I learned how to install drain and dishwasher dispensers. I worked with employees toiling on city streets at six in the morning. I know how school lunchrooms function. The unsung heroes with burns on their hands and arms, sweating in kitchens without air conditioning, have gained my respect.

I consider myself fortunate to have toured Jack Daniels Old Time Distillery in Lynchburg, TN, Mayfield Dairy, and Coca Cola's headquarters in Atlanta. I've visited Brach's Candy Factory and McKee Foods, producers of Little Debbie Snack Cakes, located in Collegedale, TN. In the late '80s, in the town of Collegedale, home of Southern Adventist University, I encountered with delight my first all-natural and vegetarian market.

I have counted Weigel's Dairy and scores of other industries, including carpet manufacturers, lumber companies, and millwrights, among my customers.

Engineers escorted me inside their plants to observe operations. I've collected several hard hats given to me by these men. Maintenance supervisors explained where they needed special gear oil and hydraulic fluid. If an industrial wastewater plant was operated on site, their operators sometimes purchased products from me.

Customers included Knoxville Zoo, where employees allowed me to drive through the back gate to visit their engineers. Frequently one of the staff gave me a tour around the zoo to show me a new animal exhibit not yet open to the public.

Dollywood Park in Pigeon Forge became another frequent destination. I drove in via a side entrance to the train depot. Engineers purchased grease from my company to lubricate their trains and hand cleaner for greasy hands.

Golf course maintenance personnel drove me through courses in golf carts, allowing me to collect soil samples to determine which herbicides would work best. One utility plant gave me a ride in the cherry picker on their bucket truck, and maintenance employees taught me how to drive a backhoe.

Once, I received a surprise call from the Smithsonian in Washington, D.C. The purchasing agent had heard I carried a new ice-melting compound that was green in color. Designed to blend in with foliage, this product would not harm grass or concrete. He faxed me an order for several hundred dollars' worth. My life in a sales day never became ho-hum.

Experiences and knowledge gained in trekking thousands of miles throughout southern Appalachia have instilled in me a longing for adventure. Confidence gained from cold-calls has certainly helped in other aspects of my life.

A Cancun, Mexico, vacation with my friend, Darlene, brought us an unwanted visitor in 1988 in the form of Hurricane Gilbert. During this weather extreme, I was frightened, but no one was injured because our condo was well built. We obeyed the rules: tape the windows, and go to a safe room. We drug mattresses to the hallway, filled bathtubs with water for later use, and tried to remain calm.

After the storm passed, Darlene and I realized we had nothing to eat except canned vegetables and cold tortilla shells. We had used all the saved bathtub water to flush the toilet in our condo bathroom. My chemical training proved helpful in finding water. I located the maintenance supervisor and offered him a few pesos to take us to his basement, where he loaned us buckets. From the sump we collected as much water as we would need to flush toilets. We found food by standing in line for a cold buffet at the Cancun Hilton as if we were their guests. Years of selling products from cookies to chemicals have taught me to adapt to most situations without complaint and to find the adventure in them.

My family, unable to reach me, experienced concern for my safety. A week after the storm, planes began offering flights and we returned home, dirty and hungry.

Later that same week, I stopped to visit my customer, the Engineering Department at St. Mary's Hospital in Knoxville. Engineers and office personnel in the department heard of my plight and welcomed me with banners, learn-how-to-swim coupons, and a plastic float. One of the many reasons I loved my customers

Hundreds of roads, thousands of people composed my Appalachian journey. James Michener said, "If you reject the food, ignore the customs, fear the religion, and avoid the people, you might better stay home."

I'm glad I didn't stay home.

Epilogue
A Life in the Twilight of a Lady Salesman

Who knows whether in retirement I shall be tempted to the last infirmity of mundane minds, which is to write a book.

—Geoffrey Fisher, clergyman

My life has changed since my retirement from sales, and I am often restless. I sometimes visit previous customers—those who haven't died or retired. I subscribe to trade magazines from the chemical industry, although they now arrive via e-mail.

Cold-calling filled me with self-doubts in the first few years, yet it instilled me with a fearless spirit. Thanks to my childhood adventures with my family and subsequent adventures in selling, almost no undertaking is too risky for me.

Hawaii has twice been my vacation destination. Although no one in my group ventured on a snorkeling trip, I rode a local bus to devote a beautiful day to viewing tropical fish with delight. Ignoring cautions from friends, I traveled by helicopter to nearby Hawaiian Islands to swim and snorkel in the Pacific Ocean my favorite way—alone. Underwater exploits without the companionship of co-workers or family took my mind back to years of traveling alone.

Morocco has called me back twice since living there in the 1970's. Family members with me were uneasy about my exploring medinas, markets, and the Kasbah alone. A *petit* taxi provided my ride to revisit many Moroccan memories.

Brass in Moroccan shop

A rental car helped me get lost in the outskirts of Rabat and the mountains of Spain. I could manage the language after getting lost in Morocco, but residents of Estepona, Spain, were unable to understand "Where am I?" in my miserable Spanish with a Tennessee drawl. I enjoyed scores of flea markets and cafés in both countries, and, by dark, I found my way back to our rented condos.

My dear friend, Eleanor, and I purchased a trip to Shanghai, China, through her flight attendant daughter. We spent a week in this exciting city. Being lost in a country where signs and directions don't use our alphabet is unnerving. A simple walk to a Chinese grocery store found us in alleys and parks with no apparent help in sight until I remembered a hotel brochure in my purse. A local gentleman recognized the hotel picture. He motioned for us to follow him, and, upon arrival at our destination, he left us with a smile and a bow.

One year, my son's friend asked him to cater his wedding in New Jersey, so I drove him, dropped him off at the groom's house, and spent a memorable two days touring nearby Philadelphia alone. Another time, I drove to Philadelphia to attend a meeting, driving twelve hours alone.

"Mom, you can't do these things" are words to acknowledge and then ignore.

My adventurous nature was the cause of a number of stomach maladies while in foreign countries. Ignoring warnings from travel companions, I seldom refused to purchase food from street vendors, finding that the best food available sometimes came from a cart.

I anticipate more adventures, perhaps with my grandchildren. I recently broke my arm while teaching my granddaughter, Estella, how to climb a tree, so I may have to tone down the physical adventures a little.

The life of a sales rep offered freedom and the opportunity for a decent income, but my sales life at times found me lonely. Days spent either listening or talking about products and evenings tending to paperwork left little time to nurture friendships. Phone calls from friends often remained unanswered. I offered inane excuses when refusing invitations to meet for dinner and a movie.

My reserved nature adapted to customers, depending on their personalities. I learned early in my sales career to keep my own council and to listen to a customer's needs and opinions. If my buyer praised a candidate for office that I disliked, well, okay with me. If she loved bleach, if he believed dinosaurs walked the earth with men, who was I to disagree? My job was not to argue, but to make a sale. Folks I met while in sales didn't require my opinion on matters not related to products. I once read that learning to sell is simply acting, so, in the beginning, I pretended to be an actor to protect my feelings.

In listening to others for a third of my lifetime, I lost my own voice. I wonder, is it too late to find that voice, and use it?

***

Many nights, my dreams are of sales, and I carry my sample case into unknown accounts in unfamiliar towns, demonstrating various products. I dream of calling suppliers to order products, of applying for sales jobs, of attempting to convince the interviewer that my age won't matter. I wake up, and I'm not sure if its sadness or relief I feel.

Sources

1. Dial, Wylene P. "The Dialect of the Appalachian People." A copyrighted publication of West Virginia Archives and History, Vol. 30, No. 2 (1969): 463-71.

2. Inc. Foxfire Fund. *Foxfire 7*, Edited by Paul. F. Gillespie. New York: Anchor Press (1982): 25.

Made in the USA
Charleston, SC
27 July 2013